The *food* Manual

Published in January 2009.

British Library Cataloguing in Publication Data:
A catalogue record for this book is available
from the British Library.

ISBN 978 1 84425 512 2

Published by Haynes Publishing,
Sparkford, Yeovil, Somerset BA22 7JJ, UK
Tel: 01963 442030 Fax: 01963 440001
Int. tel: +44 1963 442030
Int. fax: +44 1963 440001
E-mail: sales@haynes.co.uk
Website: www.haynes.co.uk

Haynes North America Inc.
861 Lawrence Drive, Newbury Park,
California 91320, USA

Printed and bound in Great Britain
by J. H. Haynes & Co. Ltd, Sparkford

The *food* Manual

YOUR GUIDE TO NUTRITION AND HEALTHY EATING

CARINA NORRIS

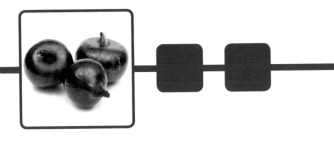

Contents

Introduction

Over two thousand years ago the Greek physician, Hippocrates, said: 'Let food be your medicine.' Wise words indeed. But sadly, since the Ancient Greeks, we've lost our way, and nowadays many of us could be digging our own graves with our knives and forks as unhealthy food becomes our downfall.

Scary talk, perhaps, but it's hard to understate the importance of the food we eat. It's not just 'fuel'. We need food to make the very building blocks of our cells and to keep our bodies functioning properly.

Rather than dwelling on the negatives of junk food and poor eating habits, let's concentrate on the benefits of good nutrition. Eat well, and your body will run more smoothly and be more resistant to whatever the world throws at it. You'll feel better, and in the long term you'll increase your life expectancy. You'll also enjoy those extra years more, because you'll be healthier.

Good nutrition isn't about denial – it's about balance and moderation. Good food can give you a lot of pleasure. Eating well isn't hard work – you won't have to spend hours in the kitchen, or trail around health food stores or scour the internet looking for exotic ingredients. You won't have to give up snacks (they're a vital part of a healthy diet), or even chocolate or alcohol. Neither will healthy eating cost a fortune – in fact, since it revolves around 'real' ingredients, such as fruit, vegetables, meat, fish and grains, rather than highly processed manufactured goods with their huge mark-up in price, you could end up saving money. And in case you're worrying about having to fork out for expensive pills and supplements, most people can get all the nutrients from their diet. (Only certain people need extra nutrients – for example, pregnant women, or vegans – and this book will cover those situations later.)

1 What's in it for me?

A poor diet has many negative effects. A healthy diet, on the other hand, helps you to fulfil your potential, giving you many benefits:

■ Plenty of energy
■ Enables you to achieve a healthy weight that's right for you
■ Strong immunity, to help prevent you from picking up every cough and cold that's going around
■ Better concentration
■ Smooth skin, glossy hair and healthy nails
■ Better circulation
■ Decreased risk of chronic diseases such as type 2 diabetes, cancer, heart disease and osteoporosis

2 What is a 'poor diet'?

It's strange, but many of us in the Western world today are suffering from overnutrition and undernutrition at the same time.

Overnutrition
We eat more than we need (especially unhealthy fatty foods) so we gain weight, putting us at risk from a whole host of conditions, from heart disease and cancer to type 2 diabetes and arthritis. And by eating too much saturated fat and salt, we increase our risk even more.

Undernutrition
A lot of the foods we eat are 'nutrient poor' – high in calories, fat and sugar, but low in nutrients such as vitamins and minerals. At the same time, we don't eat enough of the fruit, vegetables and 'wholefoods' that are naturally rich in vitamins and minerals, so we miss out on vital nutrients.

Nutrient-dense versus nutrient-poor foods
A healthy diet is based on 'nutrient-dense' foods rather than 'nutrient-poor' ones. What's the difference? Nutrient-dense foods are packed with nutrients and are generally lower in calories. Nutrition-wise, you get more 'bang for your buck'! Nutrient-poor foods have more calories for the amount of food, and are usually lower in nutrients. Nutrition-wise, they're 'wasted calories'.

To give you an example, let's compare an orange with a Danish pastry. They're about the same size, but the nutrient-dense orange is low in calories and a fantastic source of vitamins (such as vitamin C) and fibre, which is good for your digestion and helps to sustain you between meals. The pastry, however, is low in vitamins and minerals, and contains virtually no fibre. Also, it's high in fat (especially unhealthy saturated fat) and sugar, and although it has about three times the calories of the orange, you'll soon be hungry again.

Eating nutrient-dense foods also means you can eat *more* food without putting on weight!

Nutrient-poor foods are a waste of space in our diets, and all too often they crowd out the nutrient-dense alternatives. We fill up on fizzy drinks, pizzas and fries, leaving no room for healthier foods such as fruit and vegetables. And as a double-whammy for our health, as well as depriving us of the nutrients we need, nutrient-poor foods threaten our health by sending our intakes of food components such as fat and sugar, soaring.

Armed with the knowledge in this book, you'll be able to tell the difference, and making healthy choices will become second nature.

Empty calories
Alcohol and sugary foods are often termed 'empty calories' because they are so low in nutritional value but pack a hefty calorific punch.

Getting started
Nutrition is a science, but don't be daunted – healthy eating is easy. You don't need to worry about learning the name of every obscure nutrient and how much of it you get in every single food. It's much more practical just to learn the basic principles. And that's where this book comes in, giving you the knowledge to enable you to figure out whether a food is likely to be good for you or not. It's all about making the best choices when you're shopping, cooking or eating out.

If you're not eating as well as you should, you'll want to train yourself to replace the foods that are high in fat, salt and sugar with healthier alternatives.

Generally the best technique is to clean up your diet as fast as possible – that way you'll see the benefits more quickly, and results are your best motivator. But don't attempt to go cold turkey – if you're used to living on fast food and takeaways, diving headlong into a regime of wholemeal noodles and buckwheat is a recipe for failure.

Here are just a few relatively painless ways to 'kick start' your new way of eating.

Some things to reduce:
■ If you must have takeaways, or eat at fast food joints, cut down on the frequency. Do without them if possible.
■ Eat less processed food, and make more of your meals from scratch. You'll not only lower your intake of fat, salt and sugar, not to mention artificial additives, but you'll probably also increase your intake of starchy carbohydrates, vitamins and minerals.
■ Stop adding salt at the table and reduce the salt you add during cooking.
■ Cut down the number of teaspoons of sugar you take in tea and coffee.

And some substitutions:
■ Snack on fruit and unsalted nuts rather than crisps or chocolate.
■ Have some pulse-based (beans or lentils) dishes instead of meat-based dishes, and slash the meals' fat and calorie counts at a stroke, as well as boosting your intake of fibre, along with several important vitamins, minerals and other nutrients.
■ Swap 'regular' versions of foods such as baked beans, tomato ketchup, mayonnaise and salad cream for low-fat, low-sugar and low-salt versions.
■ Grill, steam or poach food rather than frying.
■ Switch from white to wholemeal bread and pasta, and have brown rice instead of white.

Most people find that when they're exposed to temptation or stress, for example at Christmas or when they've have a particularly tough day, they tend to resort to old, bad eating habits. These are the times when you're more likely to fall off the wagon and give in to a sweet, sticky treat, a drink too many, or some unhealthy fast food.

Don't beat yourself up about it! It's not the end of the world, and tomorrow is a new day.

Try to live by the '80–20 rule'. Eat healthily for 80% of the time, and you can afford to relax a little for the other 20%. The 80–20 rule works with human nature, rather than against it. You're allowed treats and lapses – you're more likely to be able to stick to your healthy eating regime in the long run that way than if you feel you'll never be able to have chocolate, crisps or ice cream ever again. Try to eat according to the 80–20 rule or, even better, the 90–10 rule.

Chapter 1

The nuts and bolts of a healthy diet

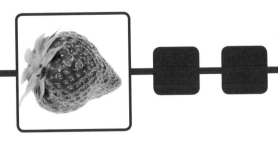

Many people think of food as 'fuel' for the body. That's true, but food is much more than that.

Food provides:
- ■ Energy for life – moving about, keeping us warm – as well as for the thousands of processes that tick away below the surface of our bodies
- ■ Raw materials for growth and repair
- ■ Defence against stress and illness (supporting the immune system)

Everybody needs what are known as macronutrients: protein, carbohydrates (including fibre) and fats. These are needed in quantities of grams each day.

We also all need micronutrients in smaller quantities – milligrams (mg) or even micrograms (μg) – but they're still vital. These are the vitamins, minerals and other beneficial natural chemicals in our food. Then there's water, often overlooked, but essential for life.

1 Energy (calories)

Before getting started on actual nutrients, we need to know about calories.

Firstly, calories are not the enemy! A calorie (kcal) is simply a unit of energy, and energy is a fundamental requirement for life, enabling us to move about, grow, digest food, keep warm, and even to think (the brain is a very energy-hungry organ). The problem comes when we consume too many calories and they are stored as fat.

Unfortunately, many foods are high in calories but low in nutrients – the 'nutrient-poor' foods mentioned in Chapter 1. We call the worst of these foods 'empty calories' – in other words they contain calories, but little or no other nutritional benefit. Eat too many of these kind of foods and you'll hit your recommended calorie intake before you meet your nutritional targets.

But don't let yourself get bogged down with calories. They're useful for comparisons (seeing how people need more energy at certain ages, for example) and to help you decide between different brands of food in the supermarket. But that's it. Eat a healthy, balanced diet and you won't need to worry about calorie-counting.

Age (years)	Calorie requirements (kcal)	
	Boys/Men	Girls/Women
Children		
7–10	1,970	1,740
11–14	2,200	1,845
15–18	2,755	2,110
Adults		
19–59	2,550	1,920
60–74	2,355	1,900
75+	2,100	1,810

These are the estimated average requirements for children and adults, but it's important to remember that people will have different requirements according to their activity levels, state of health, and even their genes – there's no such thing as an 'average' person!

2 Protein

Protein is needed for body growth (building new cells) and repair (manufacturing new cells to repair tissues as they wear out). It's also needed for healing when the body is damaged. Protein can be used as a source of energy, but it's much harder for the body to obtain energy from protein than from carbohydrates or fat, so it's very much used as a last resort when the body runs low on fuel.

Protein is made up of sub-units called amino acids, the building blocks of life. When you eat proteins, they are broken down by the digestive system into their constituent amino acids, which can then be absorbed and used by the body to make new proteins.

Protein has a huge variety of functions – these are just a few:
- Building muscle tissue
- Structural proteins, such as those found in skin, hair and fingernails
- Many hormones
- Many enzymes, used to regulate chemical reactions in the body
- Antibodies, needed for immunity
- Making haemoglobin, used to transport oxygen in the blood.

How much protein do we need?

Protein needs

	Age (years)	Protein (g per day)
Men	19–50	56
	50+	53
Women	19–50	45
	50+	47

Extra protein needs

Women need extra protein during pregnancy and breastfeeding. Children have proportionally higher protein needs than adults. Most children need approximately 1g of protein for every kilogram of their bodyweight – adults only require 0.75g of protein per kilogram of bodyweight.

More protein is also required when you are recovering from illness or injury. Contrary to popular belief, people who are doing a lot of exercise don't necessarily need a 'high-protein diet'. They do, however, need to eat more food, and if they are eating a healthy balanced diet, their protein requirements will be adequately supplied. Only professional athletes and those on specialised and supervised training regimes should tinker with seriously increasing their protein intakes, and should take advice from a nutrition professional.

Most people in the developed world eat more protein than they need, and deficiency is very rare. The average daily intake of protein in the UK is 88g for men and 64g for women.

More often it's the quality, not the quantity, of protein in our diets that causes problems. You need to ensure that your protein comes from sources that are low in unhealthy saturated fats, salt and additives.

Good protein sources include:

Animal sources:
- Lean meat
- Poultry
- Fish
- Eggs
- Low-fat dairy products (eg milk, cheese (including cottage cheese) and yoghurt)

Non-animal sources:
- Pulses (beans and lentils)
- Nuts (eg almonds, Brazil nuts, hazelnuts, cashew nuts)
- Seeds (eg sunflower seeds, sesame seeds, pumpkin seeds)
- Quorn, and soya products such as tofu and soya meat-substitutes
- Wholegrains also contain a small amount of protein.

In the UK we get approximately two-thirds of our protein from animal sources, such as meat, fish, eggs and dairy foods. A further quarter comes from cereal products (such as bread and other products made from flour) and most of the remainder from nuts and pulses. Nuts and pulses are actually much richer in protein than cereals – it's the amount of cereal products we eat that skews their importance as protein providers.

Animal protein versus vegetable protein

Both animal and non-animal protein sources have their own advantages and disadvantages. Animal protein has a higher 'biological value', meaning that it's easier for the body to use. However, it contains saturated fat, which we should minimise in our diets. Vegetarian protein sources have a lower biological value, so they're harder for the body to use. But they lack the bad saturated fat, and many also contain healthy unsaturated fats. They also contain fibre, which is good for digestion and benefits cholesterol levels, making them heart-healthy too.

Probably the healthiest option is to get your protein from as wide a variety of protein sources as possible, with an emphasis on vegetarian sources.

Protein to choose and protein to avoid

Cook quality meat yourself, rather than relying on processed foods – they're generally much higher in fat and salt, and padded out with added bulkers and fillers, water, sugar and artificial preservatives and other chemical additives.

Give these a miss:
- Sausages (except low-fat ones as an occasional treat) and sausage rolls
- Burgers (except low-fat ones, and those you make yourself)
- Frankfurters
- Salami, pepperoni and other 'fancy' sausages
- Black pudding and white pudding
- Scotch eggs
- Pork pies
- Chicken nuggets (except for homemade, or those made from chicken breast in a low-fat, low-salt crumb coating)
- Re-formed meat and poultry slices. These are made from minced-up meat, which may not be good quality, reformed and sliced. Look for meat that's just labelled 'sliced' – then you know it hasn't been processed.
- Breaded products made from 're-formed' chicken, fish and meat
- Deep-fried fish

If you enjoy eating meat and other animal products, you can minimise the saturated fat in your protein foods by:
- Avoiding 'processed protein' (see box)
- Trimming the fat from meat (before cooking if possible)
- Buying lean meat and mincing it yourself – bought mince often has a lot of fat minced in
- Removing the skin from chicken and other poultry – this is where you'll find most of the fat
- Choosing low-fat dairy products such as semi-skimmed or skimmed milk, low-fat yogurt and fromage frais, low-fat spreads and low-fat cheese (including cottage cheese, an excellent protein source).

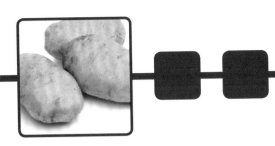

3 Carbohydrates

Carbohydrates include starches and sugars, and are what the body runs on. They come in a variety of forms, from simple to complex, depending on how many sugar units they're composed of and how they're put together.

■ Complex carbohydrates = starchy carbohydrates, made up of long chains of sugar units

■ Simple carbohydrates = sugars.

How much carbohydrate do we need?
As our body's main energy source, carbohydrates should make up a minimum of 40 per cent of our calories. Almost all of that should come from starchy, complex carbohydrates, and preferably wholegrains. Only 10 per cent or less should be from sugary food.

Athletes, and people with very high physical activity levels, need a higher proportion of calories from carbohydrates – about 60–70 per cent. And once again, they should concentrate on the healthy wholegrain carbohydrates.

Choosing the best carbohydrates
Starchy carbohydrates are better for you than simple sugars, but some starches are better than others, because of their 'stabilising' effect on your blood sugar and therefore energy levels (see also Chapter 7). The best starches are the wholegrains, which are unrefined and also have

naturally high levels of vitamins and minerals (especially the B vitamins). Refined (white) starches are less healthy.

This means that you should go for wholemeal and wholegrains when you choose starchy foods. Pick wholemeal bread, wholemeal pasta, porridge oats, brown rice, bulgur wheat, millet, buckwheat and quinoa rather than the white versions of bread, rice and pasta.

The problems with sugar

What's so unhealthy about sugar?

- It can contribute to tooth decay, especially when eaten between meals
- Sugary foods are often described as 'empty calories' because they supply calories but little or no nutritional benefit
- Sugary treats can crowd out more nutritious foods from people's diets
- Many sugary foods are also often high in fat – think of chocolate, ice cream and other desserts, biscuits and cakes
- Because they taste so good, and are less filling than starchy foods, they don't sustain you for long.

But there's no such thing as a totally 'bad' food – and sugars are no exception. It's a question of how much, how often, and the kind of sugars you eat.

Can sugars be good for you?

When people talk about how unhealthy sugars are, they're generally referring to refined, table sugar, or sucrose, the kind that's added to tea and coffee, in cooking, and processed foods. But not all sugars are man-made. There are 'natural' sugars, too, for example the fructose (fruit sugar) found in fruit, and the lactose (milk sugar) present in milk.

These natural sugars are healthier than refined sugar. They are less quickly absorbed by the body (because the fibre in the fruit and the fat in the milk means it takes longer for the body to break down and release the energy), so they

sustain you for longer. And in fruit and milk these natural sugars also come packaged with a whole variety of other nutrients. When you eat fruit you're also taking in vitamins, minerals and fibre, and when you drink milk, you also get protein, calcium, and vitamins A and D.

Fruit juice is an interesting case. On the one hand, it's an easy way to get the vitamin benefits of fresh fruit, as you can count one 150ml glass of fruit juice towards your 'five-a-day' fruit and vegetable target. But fruit juice is also high in sugars (albeit natural ones) in a quick release form, and it's acidic, so it can damage your teeth.

Stick to one glass of pure fruit juice per day, and if you want a fruity tasting drink the rest of the time, dilute pure juice with water. And always check the label when buying fruit juice. Look for 100% pure juice with no added sugar or sweeteners, rather than 'fruit juice drink'.

How much sugar do we need?

We don't 'need' any simple sugar in our diet, because our bodies are perfectly able to break down other foods to provide energy.

These are the recommended maximum sugar intakes – less is better:

Average man	50g (approx. 10 teaspoons)
Average woman	47g (approx. 9 teaspoons)
Primary school age children	
Boys	46g
Girls	44g
Secondary school age children	
Boys	62g
Girls	49g

Teenagers have higher figures because adolescents have very high energy (calorie) intakes, and the maximum sugar recommendations are calculated as a percentage of this.

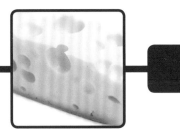

4 Fats

Too much fat is unhealthy. It's packed with calories (no other food group is higher), so it can cause you to become overweight or obese, which is bad for anyone's health. And some kinds of fats can increase your risk of diseases such as heart disease, cancer, stroke and even Alzheimer's disease.

The recommended maximum fat intake is for us to get no more than 35 per cent of our calories from fat (and more cautious nutritionists say that 30 per cent is a better target).

Recommended maximum total fat intake

For an average man: 99g
For an average woman: 75g

Remember this isn't just the butter or spread you put on your toast, and the oil in your frying pan. As well as the white fat on meat and in and below the skin of poultry, fat is concealed in even lean-looking meat, in eggs, milk and other dairy products, in salad dressings and sauces, as well as in a huge range of manufactured foods.

But it's wrong to demonise fat – everyone needs a certain amount in their diet in order to remain healthy. And some kinds of fat have health benefits of their own.

People need some fat in their diets for several reasons:

- Energy – fat from our diets, and fat stored in our body, can be broken down to provide fuel
- A thin layer of body fat is needed to protect our vital organs such as the kidneys and liver
- To supply fat-soluble vitamins and to enable us to absorb and use them (vitamins A, D, E, and K)
- To build cell membranes
- To produce essential hormones
- For healthy brain function
- To maintain the oil content of the skin and hair – a diet that is too low in fat can lead to flaky skin and dry hair.

It's the kind of fat as well as the amount that's important. Saturated fats are harmful to health, so you should minimise them in your diet. Hydrogenated, or 'trans', fats are even worse. But the unsaturated fats (the so-called monounsaturates and polyunsaturates, which

include the omega-3 and omega-6 essential fatty acids) are positively healthy. You just need to concentrate on the 'good fats' and minimise the 'bad fats'.

You may have heard of 'lipids' – this is simply another term for fats and oils.

What you need to know about cholesterol

Too much cholesterol can clog and damage your arteries, increasing your risk of heart disease and stroke. But cholesterol is also vital for our body's normal functioning – it forms part of our cell membranes and nerves, and it's needed to make hormones. For many years we were advised to avoid high-cholesterol foods (such as eggs and prawns), but we now know that the cholesterol produced by our bodies plays a far more important role in determining our blood cholesterol level.

The amount of cholesterol our bodies make is affected by a variety of factors, including what we eat. So the best way to try to avoid clogged arteries is to avoid the foods that stimulate our bodies to make cholesterol.

To complicate things further, there are good and bad kinds of cholesterol. When we talk about 'lowering your cholesterol levels', that's generally the total level, or alternatively the level of the 'bad' form of cholesterol.

- LDL (or 'bad') -cholesterol hangs around in the blood circulation and is taken up by the artery walls, leading to thickening known as atherosclerosis, or 'furring' of the arteries. Clogged arteries restrict the blood flow, contributing to heart problems such as high blood pressure, angina and heart attacks. They also increase your risk of stroke.
- HDL (or 'good') -cholesterol shuttles cholesterol in the blood to the liver where it can be broken down. HDL helps protect you from heart disease and strokes.

Saturated fats

A diet high in saturated fats increases your risk of:
- Heart disease
- Stroke
- Certain cancers
- Alzheimer's disease.

Saturated fats increase your levels of the harmful LDL form of cholesterol, which can contribute to clogged arteries.

Saturated fats are usually solid at room temperature and almost all come from animal products – examples include butter and lard, and the fat found in meat and cheese. Milk and yoghurt also contain saturated fat, contained in tiny globules.

Non-animal foods generally contain the 'healthier' fats (see below). The few examples of saturated plant fats are palm oil (or palm nut oil), coconut oil and cocoa butter (used in chocolate). However, coconut oil and cocoa butter are believed to have some health benefits that partially cancel out the effects of them being saturated fats. But that's no excuse to overindulge in chocolate or rich Thai curries!

You'll find palm oil in a lot of manufactured foods, including biscuits, cakes, pastry and chocolate bars, so check the label. And if it just says 'vegetable fat' it's probably coconut or palm oil.

You don't need saturated fats. It's easy to get all the fats you need from unsaturated sources, which are much healthier.

That's not to say you have to totally avoid saturated fats – after all, they're found in plenty of foods like lean meat, eggs and dairy products, which are healthy in moderation, especially when you choose the low-fat options. Just make sure that most of your fat comes from the healthy, unsaturated sources.

Saturated fat-reducing swaps

High saturated fat	Lower saturated fat
Processed meat products (eg sausages)	'Real' cuts of lean meat
Red meats (eg beef, lamb)	White meats (chicken, turkey)
Farmed meats (eg beef, lamb, pork)	Game (eg venison, game birds)
Fatty poultry (duck, goose)	Low-fat poultry (chicken, turkey)
Meals based around meat	Meals based around beans and lentils
Curries	Tandoori and tikka dishes
Creamy pasta sauces	Tomato-based pasta sauces
Puff, flaky and shortcrust pastry	Filo pastry
Full-fat milk	Semi-skimmed or skimmed milk
Full-fat, luxury or Greek yogurt	Low-fat or fat-free yogurt
Full-fat cream cheese	Low-fat soft cheese, or cottage cheese
Full fat mascarpone cheese	Low-fat quark
Cheddar, Cheshire, Stilton, Roquefort	Camembert, Edam, Brie, Mozzarella
Cream with desserts	Low fat natural yogurt, quark or fromage frais
Ice cream	Frozen yogurt

Hydrogenated fats

These unhealthy fats are made for the food industry, by adding hydrogen to otherwise healthy oils, to turn them into solid fats, and to increase their shelf-life. They're also extremely cheap to make.

Hydrogenated (and partially hydrogenated) fats and oils are the main source of 'trans' fats in our diets. Trans fats contribute to the same kind of health problems as saturated fats – they can lead to weight gain, block your arteries and increase your risk of heart disease and strokes.

In addition, because they're very similar in structure to the healthy unsaturated fats, the body sometimes mistakenly uses them instead of their healthier counterparts. And a body incorporating trans fats into its cells and using them as fuel has a higher health risk than one running on healthy unsaturated fat.

You'll find hydrogenated and partially hydrogenated fats (and therefore trans fats) in a variety of processed foods, including ready-meals, sauces in jars and packets, instant drinks and instant soups, cakes and cake mixes, biscuits, pastries, sweets, desserts, pudding mixes, some ice creams, chocolates and chocolate bars. They are also used for frying in some fast food restaurants.

Fortunately, many brands and restaurants are removing hydrogenated fats from their products, and many of the supermarkets are taking them out of their own-brand foods – you need to check the labels.

Unsaturated fats

While you need to make sure you don't overdo your total fat intake, unsaturated fats have important health benefits. It's vital to have a certain amount of them in your diet.

Unsaturated fats are generally oils – liquid at room temperature. Almost all vegetable oils are unsaturated, as are fish oils (more about those later).

Unsaturated fats are divided into:
- Polyunsaturated fats
- Monounsaturated fats

Polyunsaturated fats

Polyunsaturated fats, or 'polyunsaturates', lower your levels of the harmful LDL form of cholesterol, and this reduces your heart risk. But they also reduce your levels of beneficial HDL-cholesterol, which cancels out some of the benefits.

However, many polyunsaturates (especially the essential fatty acids) have other health benefits. They're involved in growth and development, and in brain function, so they're definitely important nutrients in your diet.

Good sources of polyunsaturated fats include sunflower oil, safflower oil, soybean oil and corn oil. The omega-3 and omega-6 essential fatty acids are also polyunsaturates, and you'll find these in oily fish, nuts and seeds.

Monounsaturated fats

Generally speaking, these are the healthiest type of fat. They're good for your heart and may help prevent cancer and other chronic illnesses. Monounsaturated fats help to lower your levels of 'bad' LDL-cholesterol. But unlike polyunsaturates, they have the added advantage of not lowering your 'good' HDL-cholesterol.

Olive oil, canola oil, rapeseed oil, peanut oil and sesame oil, and also avocados and olives, are high in monounsaturated fats, or 'monounsaturates'.

Essential fatty acids

We need fats, or 'fatty acids', for a huge range of processes and to build our cell membranes. Fatty acids come in many varieties. Most of them can be made by the body by breaking down and reassembling other fats – except for a group of polyunsaturated fats, the so-called 'essential fatty acids' or EFAs. We need to supply these ready made in our diets.

There are two main kinds of EFAs:
- Omega-3 EFAs
- Omega-6 EFAs

Omega-3 EFAs

Omega-3s are good for your heart and brain, and help prevent inflammatory diseases.

They have been found to help:
- Reduce your risk of cardiovascular disease (heart disease and stroke).
- Manage and prevent inflammatory diseases like rheumatoid arthritis, Crohn's disease, ulcerative colitis and lupus.
- Prevent and fight depression.
- Prevent dementia, and perhaps even the age-related 'slow-down' of mental processes.

The omega-3s are the 'fishy fats'. The best sources are oily fish, such as salmon, trout, mackerel, sardines, pilchards and herring. Fresh oily fish is best, but canned oily fish is a reasonable source, except for tuna, as the omega-3s are destroyed when tuna is canned.

There are a few vegetarian sources of omega-3s, but these are less easy for the body to use. The best vegetarian omega-3 sources are flax seeds and their oil, but you'll also find smaller amounts in pumpkin seeds and walnuts. You can also buy vegetarian omega-3 supplements, sourced from micro-algae.

Omega-6 EFAs

The health benefits of these essential fats are similar to those of the omega-3s, though not quite as dramatic. They are good for your skin, helping to keep it smooth and supple, and preventing dryness. They may also reduce our risk of type 2 diabetes. New research has shown promising results for omega-6s in improving skin conditions such as eczema.

Omega-6s are found in nuts and seeds, as well as some vegetable oils – corn oil, sunflower oil and safflower oil.

Getting the EFA balance right

If you eat too much omega-6 in comparison to omega-3, this cancels out some of the health benefits.

Most people's diets are skewed in favour of omega-6s, because omega-6s are found in commonly eaten foods such as chicken, eggs, sunflower oil and fat spreads. We find it harder to get enough omega-3s, which come from oily fish, and from flax seeds and their oil.

Don't worry too much about getting the balance precisely right, but make an effort to increase the amount of omega-3s in your diet. That should help even the balance and take you close to the target.

Omega-3 supplements

If you hate oily fish, you can boost your intake with a good quality omega-3 or fish oil supplement (make sure you buy fish oil, not fish liver oil or cod liver oil – this is very different). You can also buy special omega-3 enriched foods such as eggs or milk – but you generally have to eat a large amount in order to get the benefits, so check the label for the amount per serving and compare it with what you'd get from supplements, which are generally a far more economical option.

Omega-3s and cardiovascular disease

Ensuring you get plenty of omega-3s in your diet can reduce your risk of the big killer cardiovascular diseases – those that affect your heart and circulatory system.

Omega-3 EFAs can:

■ Keep your cholesterol levels under control
They lower your levels of 'bad' LDL-cholesterol
They raise your levels of 'good' HDL-cholesterol
■ Make your blood less 'sticky', and so less likely to produce life-threatening blood clots
■ Lower your blood pressure
■ Help maintain steady heart rhythm, preventing dangerous arrhythmias.

Omega-3s play a vital role in keeping your blood flowing smoothly around your circulatory system. Roughened, narrowed arteries are more likely to become clogged, by encouraging blood to clot at the site of damage. If this happens in the blood vessels of the heart, a heart attack occurs. If it happens in the brain, the result is a stroke (in effect, a 'brain attack'). Clots can also lodge in the major blood vessels, such as those in the legs, producing deep vein thrombosis (DVT). These clots can remain where they are, causing serious tissue damage, or become dislodged and travel to the heart or brain, with potentially lethal effects.

Omega-3s and depression

Population studies have found that depression is rarer in countries where large amounts of fish are eaten. This is thought to be at least partially due to the brain's requirement for the omega-3s found in fish, especially oily fish.

Following up these interesting findings, clinical trials have found that omega-3s can treat depression. However, the doses used were high – up to 9.6g per day. Anyone suffering from clinical depression should be under a doctor's care, and should discuss any supplements with their doctor before taking them.

Omega-3s for developing babies

Essential fatty acids are vital for the developing brain – 60 per cent of the brain's dry weight is composed of these fats. An omega-3 called docosahexaenoic acid (DHA) is particularly important in building the brain, and also for the developing eyes.

The benefits become evident when the baby grows. Recent research found that eating DHA-rich oily fish during pregnancy helped the baby's eventual language development, while another study found benefits for children's attention levels.

After the baby is born, the mother's diet continues to affect her child's brain if she is breastfeeding, as breast milk is particularly rich in those essential fatty acids.

Omega-3s and children's learning difficulties

Recent research suggests that increasing intakes of omega-3 could help children with conditions such as dyslexia, attention deficit hyperactivity disorder (ADHD) and dyspraxia. The results have been variable, but encouraging.

Omega-3s, dementias and other brain disorders

There is also a link between omega-3 EFAs and Alzheimer's disease, dementia and the gradual mental decline associated with old age. (Alzheimer's is a kind of dementia, but not all 'dementias' and forms of age-related mental decline are due to Alzheimer's.) Several large-scale population studies have found links between the amount of fish (especially oily fish) consumed and protection against these conditions. Other research found that a high intake of saturated fats seemed to increase the occurrence of dementias.

The most convincing link appears to be between high cholesterol levels and Alzheimer's, so eating a 'cholesterol-friendly' diet should help keep your brain functioning at its best.

- Reduce saturated fat
- Eat moderate amounts of unsaturated fats
- Eat foods containing soluble fibre, such as oats
- Eat plenty of fruit and vegetables.

Exercise also benefits your cholesterol level, and therefore helps your brain too.

How much fat do we need?

Total fat:	No more than 99g per day for men, 75g for women
Saturated fat:	No more than 28g per day for men, 21g for women
Polyunsaturated fats:	At least 450mg of the forms known as EPA and DHA per day (for general health). At least 500–1,800mg EPA/DHA per day (to reduce heart risk)

Get your fats right!

- Moderate or reduce your total fat intake
  Cut down on fried and processed foods
  Cut down on biscuits, cakes and pastries

- Replace saturated fats with monounsaturated fats
  Replace meat with virtually fat-free vegetarian protein (beans, lentils, etc)
  Use only small quantities of spread, and choose a low-fat unsaturated variety
  When you do fry foods, use olive oil

- Avoid trans fats
  Read the food labels and avoid hydrogenated and partially hydrogenated vegetable fats
  Avoid fast food restaurants, where the food could be deep-fried in hydrogenated oil

- Eat plenty of sustainably caught fish (at least two portions of oily fish per week) for omega-3s.
  If you don't like fish, take a fish oil or omega-3 supplement.

5 Fibre

Fibre has something of an image problem. But there's more to fibre than bowels and bran!

The recommended daily intake is 18g, but on average we only manage two-thirds of this.

Fibre:
- Keeps food moving smoothly through the digestive system, helping it to work efficiently
- Lowers your level of the 'bad' LDL-cholesterol, reducing your risk of heart disease and stroke
- Helps to keep blood sugar in balance, helping to prevent type 2 diabetes
- Reduces the risk of certain cancers, such as breast and bowel cancer
- Makes food more sustaining, helping us to resist temptation between meals
- Is good for dental health. Fibrous foods need more chewing, and this stimulates saliva flow, which in turn is good for teeth.

Fibre is a form of carbohydrate, and can be divided into three types.
- Insoluble fibre
- Soluble fibre
- Resistant starch.

Insoluble fibre

This was previously called 'roughage', but 'smoothage' would be a more appropriate term, as it smoothes food through the digestive system. Because fibre cannot be digested by human digestive enzymes, it bulks up the food in the gut, giving the intestines something to 'work on', helping to prevent diarrhoea and constipation.

The best sources of insoluble fibre are:
- Vegetables and fruit (especially the skins)
- Wholegrains (eg wholemeal bread, brown rice, brown pasta, oats, wholegrain breakfast cereals (including muesli) barley, and buckwheat
- Nuts.

Soluble fibre

This is a 'sticky' kind of fibre that binds to cholesterol in the gut, ferrying it out of the body and helping to lower blood cholesterol levels. It also slows the rate that glucose is absorbed into the bloodstream, helping to control your blood sugar levels and sustaining you between meals.

The best sources of soluble fibre are:
- Oats
- Fruit (especially apples)
- Peas, beans and lentils
- Seeds.

Resistant starch

Starchy foods are generally broken down by digestive enzymes to release energy, but a special kind of starch called resistant starch cannot be digested in this way. Instead, it passes into the large intestine where it provides 'food' for 'friendly' bacteria that inhabit the bowel. These beneficial bugs crowd out potentially harmful bacteria that reach the gut, and also help us to produce and absorb certain vitamins and minerals. They also produce so-called short-chain fatty acids (SCFAs), which could reduce your risk of colon (bowel) cancer.

In addition, in common with soluble fibre, resistant starch also slows the uptake of glucose into your bloodstream, preventing plunges and spikes in blood sugar, and helps to regulate your levels of blood lipids (fats).

The best sources of resistant starch are:
- Cooked and cooled potatoes
- Wholegrains
- Beans and lentils.

Fibre-rich foods come from plants, so incorporate plenty of fruit, vegetables, wholegrains into your diet.

But if you're not used to eating fibre, go slowly, as a sudden increase in fibre can cause a variety of digestive symptoms, including diarrhoea, constipation, discomfort and bloating. Don't be tempted to sprinkle bran on your food – it can hinder your absorption of nutrients and irritate the digestive system.

How much fibre?

Fruits

1 medium apple (with skin)	1.8g
50g dried apricots	3.2g
50g dried figs	3.5g
1 medium pear	3.1g
1 medium orange	2.5g
50g prunes	2.9g

Vegetables

1 small tin baked beans	5.5g
80g portion cooked carrots	2.0g
1 small tin red kidney beans	12.7g
80g portion cooked Brussels sprouts	2.5g
80g portion cooked broccoli	1.8g
1 medium baked potato	4.1g
4 boiled new potatoes	2.4g
80g portion cooked cabbage	1.4g

Nuts and seeds

50g peanuts	3.2g
50g almonds	3.7g
50g sunflower seeds	3.0g

Bread, grains and cereals

2 slices wholemeal bread	2.9g
2 slices granary bread	2.1g
2 slices brown bread	1.7g
Medium (240g cooked weight) serving brown pasta	8.4g
Medium (180g cooked weight) serving brown rice	1.5g
40g serving bran cereal	9.8g
40g serving bran flakes	5.2g
2 shredded wheat biscuits	4.3g
Medium (160g cooked weight) bowl cooked porridge (not instant)	1.5g

Don't forget the fluids

If you don't drink enough fluids, the fibre in your diet can't do its job. Fibre needs to absorb liquid in order to provide bulk, and without enough fluid it can cause constipation.

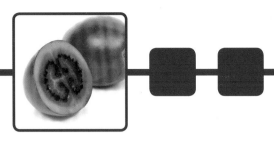

6 Vitamins and minerals

Vitamins and minerals are called micronutrients, because, unlike protein, fats, carbohydrates, and water, we only need them in minute amounts – quantities measured in thousandths or hundreds-of-thousandths of a gram per day.

But micronutrients are vital. Their roles include:

- Acting like tiny spark plugs, setting off chemical reactions essential to our body's functioning
- Metabolising food, converting carbohydrates, fats and sometimes protein into energy that the body can use
- Regulating vital body processes
- Essential for the production of hormones
- Defence of the body, supporting the immune system and protecting us from attack by harmful substances and germs

- Providing substance to our bodies. Without structural micronutrients, including many of the minerals, our bodies would literally fall to pieces.

Deficiencies in micronutrients can cause a variety of symptoms, and have two main causes:

- Primary deficiency (not getting enough in your diet)
- Secondary deficiency (not absorbing enough from your diet, due to various medical conditions, medications, smoking, excessive alcohol, or old age).

Vitamins

Vitamins can be divided into two kinds:

- Fat-soluble vitamins
  Vitamins A, D, E and K
- Water-soluble vitamins
  The B vitamins (including folic acid) and vitamin C.

Fat-soluble vitamins are stored in our body fat, so we can build up reserves of them that our bodies tap into on days when we haven't eaten enough of that particular vitamin. This very useful system is a disadvantage, however, when we eat too much of a fat-soluble vitamin over a period of time, and it can accumulate to dangerous levels. In practice, however, this rarely happens, except when people regularly take high doses of vitamins, or frequently eat a lot of very rich sources of fat-soluble vitamins (such as liver, which is extremely rich in vitamin A).

Because they dissolve in water, water-soluble vitamins are flushed out of our body in our urine. Because we don't store these vitamins, and excrete any excess, they need to be topped up every day.

mg = milligrams, or one-thousandth of a gram
μg = micrograms, or one-millionth of a gram

Fat-soluble vitamins

Vitamin	Daily requirement	Function	People at risk of deficiency	Best sources (animal)	Best sources (vegetarian)
Vitamin A	Men 700μg, women 600μg.	Plays an essential role in vision, especially night vision. Also needed for healthy skin and mucous membranes, and for a strong immune system.	People with medical conditions making it difficult to absorb fats.	Liver, oily fish, dairy products, eggs.	Green vegetables (eg spinach, broccoli), yellow and orange fruit and vegetables (eg mango, cantaloupe melon, apricots, peaches, carrots, sweet potatoes).
Vitamin D	None set for adults in the UK.	Vital for healthy bones and teeth, as it helps the body absorb and use calcium.	People with dark skin, who cover up their skin for cultural reasons, or who are housebound (these people are unable to make their own vitamin D through the action of sunlight on the skin)	Oily fish (eg salmon, sardines, mackerel), meat, eggs, dairy products.	Fortified breakfast cereals and fat spreads.
	We get most of our vitamin D from a chemical reaction caused by the action of sunlight on the skin.				
Vitamin E	None set for adults in the UK.	Needed for healthy reproductive and immune systems. An important antioxidant, protecting the body's cells from damage.	People with medical conditions making it difficult to absorb fats.	Not applicable.	Nuts and seeds and their oils, wholemeal bread, wheatgerm, avocado, spinach, broccoli.
Vitamin K	None set for adults in the UK.	Helping blood to clot, and for healthy bones (required for calcium absorption).	People taking long-term antibiotics (which kill the 'friendly' bacteria in the gut).	Eggs, fish oils, dairy products.	Green leafy vegetables, asparagus.
	Most of our vitamin K is produced naturally by harmless bacteria in our gut.				

Water-soluble vitamins

Vitamin	Daily requirement	Function	People at risk of deficiency	Best sources (animal)	Best sources (vegetarian)
Vitamin C	40mg.	Needed for a strong immune system, and for wound healing. Helps the body to absorb iron from food.	Smokers, people not eating fruit and vegetables.	Not applicable.	Fruit (especially kiwi fruit, blackcurrants, strawberries, citrus fruits), yellow and red peppers, tomatoes, Brussels sprouts.
Vitamin B1 (thiamin)	Men 1mg, women 0.8mg.	Releasing energy from food.	People who abuse alcohol.	Lean pork, liver.	Unrefined grains, nuts, seeds, fortified flour, fortified breakfast cereals.
Vitamin B2 (riboflavin)	Men 1.3mg, women 1.1mg.	Digesting and metabolising proteins and carbohydrates, resisting stress.	People with medical conditions hindering the absorption of the vitamin.	Meat (especially liver), eggs, dairy products.	Wholegrains, fortified flour and fortified breakfast cereals, dark green leafy vegetables such as watercress and spinach.
Vitamin B3 (niacin)	Men 17mg, women 13mg.	Releasing energy from food, manufacturing DNA.	People also deficient in vitamin B6 (used to convert the amino acid tryptophan to vitamin B3).	Meat, dairy products.	Flour and fortified breakfast cereals, peas.
Vitamin B6 (pyridoxine)	Men 1.4mg, women 1.2mg.	Releasing energy from food. May help to regulate mood.	Smokers, women taking oral contraceptives, people who abuse alcohol.	Liver, pork, lamb, chicken, eggs, dairy products.	Beans (especially soya beans) potatoes, brown rice, wholegrains, wheatgerm, nuts, dark green leafy vegetables.
Folic acid (another B vitamin)	200μg (more for pregnant women and those planning a baby).	Helps prevent neural tube defects in developing babies. Needed for the body to absorb nutrients effectively, and supports the immune system.	People eating diets low in vegetables, elderly people, pregnant women and those planning a baby.	Liver, eggs.	Green leafy vegetables, fortified breakfast cereals, pulses (beans and lentils), nuts, citrus fruit, apricots, broccoli, brown rice, wheatgerm.
Vitamin B12	1.5μg.	Production of red blood cells.	Vegetarians and vegans.	Red meat, fish, shellfish, eggs, dairy products.	Yeast extract, fortified breakfast cereals, fortified vegetable margarines.
	Also produced naturally by harmless bacteria in the gut.				

Minerals

Our bodies need certain minerals in order to function properly. Some contribute to our body's structure. For example, about 1.5kg (3 pounds) of our body weight is composed of the mineral calcium, almost all of it in bones and teeth. Others, such as potassium, are involved in maintaining the correct fluid balance in our blood. Selenium and copper are needed for certain chemical reactions in the body.

We obtain minerals by eating plants (which take up minerals from the soil), and eating animals (which have eaten mineral-containing plants).

Some minerals (such as structural minerals) are called major minerals and are needed in relatively large quantities. Others – the trace elements – are needed in minuscule amounts. But they're all vital for good health.

- Calcium, magnesium, phosphorus, and potassium are needed in 100s-of-milligram quantities
- Iron and zinc are needed in milligram quantities
- Iodine and selenium are needed in fractions-of-milligram quantities.

Major minerals

Mineral	Daily requirement	Function	People at risk of deficiency	Best sources (animal)	Best sources (vegetarian)
Iron	Men 8.7mg, women 14.8mg. (For a more detailed table for different ages, see Chapter 6.)	Production of healthy red blood cells to transport oxygen around the body, and prevention of anaemia.	Vegetarians and vegans (animal products are the best sources), women who have heavy periods.	Liver (the best source), kidney, red meat, chicken, eggs.	Pulses (beans and lentils), green vegetables, dried fruit (especially apricots), fortified flour.
Calcium	700mg (for a more detailed table, for different ages, see Chapter 6).	Building and maintaining healthy bones and teeth. Also needed for muscle function.	People eating insufficient dietary calcium, also those deficient in vitamins D and K.	Dairy foods, tinned fish where the bones are eaten (eg sardines and salmon).	Tofu, sesame seeds, almonds, figs, kale and other green leafy vegetables, fortified flour.
Magnesium	Men 300mg, women 270mg.	Required for healthy bones. Also helps the body deal with stress, and needed for muscle function.	People eating insufficient dietary magnesium, people abusing alcohol.	Meat, dairy products.	Green vegetables, nuts and seeds, pulses, wholegrains, dried fruits, mushrooms.
Phosphorus	550mg.	For bones and teeth. Also needed for healthy functioning of the nervous system.	People taking large doses of antacid medication over a long period (this interferes with phosphorus absorption).	Abundant in most foods, especially meat, fish, eggs, dairy products.	Abundant in most foods, especially grains, seeds, pulses, fruit and vegetables.

Trace elements

Mineral	Daily requirement	Function	People at risk of deficiency	Best sources (animal)	Best sources (vegetarian)
Zinc	Men 9.5mg, women 7mg.	Supporting the immune system and preventing infection, healthy growth and development, sperm formation in men.	People who abuse alcohol.	Oysters, meat, fish, shellfish, chicken, eggs, dairy products.	Seeds (especially pumpkin seeds), nuts, wholegrains, green leafy vegetables, pulses.
Copper	1.2mg.	Needed for healthy blood vessels, bones and nerves. Involved in deactivating harmful free radical molecules that damage cells.	People taking large doses of antacid medication over a long period (this interferes with copper absorption).	Meat (especially liver), seafood.	Wholemeal bread, nuts, seeds, green vegetables.
Selenium	Men 75μg, women 60μg.	Healthy immune system, protection against diseases including heart disease and cancer.	Smokers, people with low dietary selenium intake.	Meat, offal, fish, seafood, eggs.	Brazil nuts, sesame seeds.
Iodine	140μg.	Used to make thyroid hormones, needed for healthy growth and metabolism.	Extremely rare in the developed world.	Offal, red meat, egg yolks.	Spinach, dried fruit, pulses (especially soya), iodised salt.
Chromium	None set for the UK.	Works with insulin to regulate blood sugar levels.	Extremely rare.	Lean red meat, eggs.	Wholegrains, nuts, seeds, potatoes, broccoli, apples.

Supplements

A large proportion of us take nutritional supplements such as vitamins and minerals, but are they worth it and, more importantly, could they be harming our health?

People take supplements for a variety of reasons.

Good reasons include:
- As a 'safety net' for times when their usually healthy diet may lapse
- During certain life-stages, such as pregnancy and breastfeeding
- If they are on a special diet, such as dairy free, vegetarian or vegan
- If they don't eat at least two portions of fish (at least one of oily fish) a week – which is most of us
- Because they suffer from a condition that hampers their absorption of certain foods and nutrients, such as coeliac disease, and liver and kidney disease)
- On the advice of a health professional such as a doctor, dietician or registered nutritionist (RNutr).

Bad reasons include:
- Because they eat badly and think a supplement will compensate for this
- Because they think taking megadoses of vitamins and minerals will make them healthier.

Who needs extra vitamins?

Anyone can take a good-quality multivitamin/mineral that supplies just the recommended daily amount (no megadoses), just as a top-up, to reassure them that they're ticking all the boxes even on days when their diet falls below their usual standards.

Other people who could benefit from supplements include:

Vegetarians: They may be short on zinc and iron, as meat is the best source of these minerals. Take a good quality multivitamin/mineral supplying 100% of your recommended daily intake.

Vegans (who eat no meat, fish, dairy, eggs or honey): As well as possibly lacking zinc and iron, they may also lack calcium that's so abundant in dairy products. Animal products are the only natural food sources of vitamin B12, but fortified foods such as breakfast cereals and vegetarian spreads may be fortified with this vitamin). As with vegetarians, a 'multi' is a good idea.

People who don't eat enough fish: Not many people eat oily fish at least once weekly. A fish oil supplement (not cod liver oil) can help make up the shortfall.

Pregnant women and those planning a baby: The developing baby places a great nutritional demand on the mother, and a multivitamin designed specifically for pregnancy is a good idea. This will contain all you need, including vital folic acid. Talk to your doctor for advice, and see also Chapter 6.

Smokers: Smoking depletes your blood levels of vitamin C. Take a supplement containing 500mg.

People who don't get sunlight on their skin: If you're dark skinned, cover-up for cultural reasons or don't get outside in the sunlight, a 'multi' containing the recommended amount of vitamin D could be a good idea.

The dangers of megadoses

High doses of vitamins and minerals can be dangerous – especially the fat-soluble vitamins, which can accumulate in the body. Too much vitamin A will damage your liver, overdoing vitamin D can lead to kidney stones, and megadoses of B vitamins can cause nerve damage. Although iron deficiency is a relatively common problem, this mineral can also accumulate in the body if you overdose over a period of time. Even if you feel that you're deficient, don't take a supplement containing any more than the recommended dose without asking your GP for a blood test for iron.

How to take supplements

- Take with food, unless advised otherwise
- Don't take with tea or coffee – this hinders absorption
- Don't crush or break tablets unless the packaging says you can
- Keep supplements in a cool, dry place (not the bathroom!).

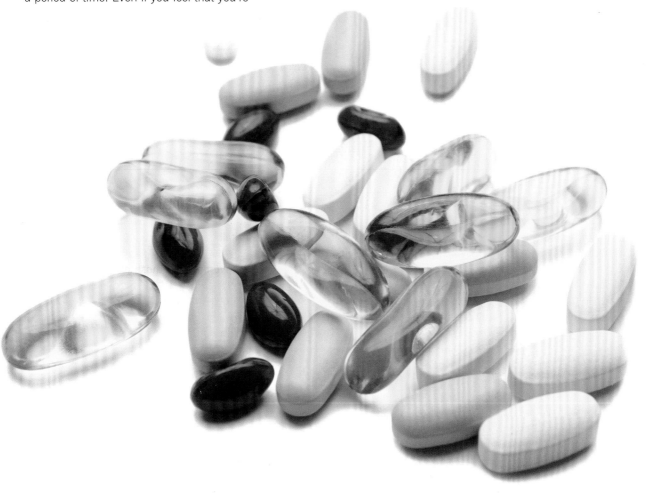

7 Putting it into practice

Healthy eating doesn't mean banning your favourite foods, giving up your social life and spending hours shopping and in the kitchen. If a glass of wine with a meal a few times a week, or the occasional chocolate, helps you to stick to more nutritious foods the rest of the time, that's fine. If you deny yourself all treats you're more likely to get resentful and miserable and give up on healthy eating as more trouble than it's worth.

Eating healthily should be a way of life – it has to be sustainable. If you want to go out for a celebration meal, there's no reason why not. Try to stick to the healthier items on the menu, but don't beat yourself up if your diet goes off the rails once in a while. You can always be 'extra good' afterwards.

Life is for living, not dieting – but there have to be *some* rules. It's all about balance.

A balanced diet for a healthy long life should contain roughly the following amounts of food per day:

- **Starchy carbohydrates:** 5–10 portions
- **Fruit**: At least 3 portions a day (more if possible)
- **Vegetables:** At least 3 portions a day (more if possible)
- **Protein foods:** 2–3 portions
- **Dairy foods:** 3 portions
- **Fatty and sugary foods:** Maximum 1 per day – try to do without!

Within those categories, you've got a lot of choice, so you can tailor your diet around the foods you like best.

Here are just a few ideas …

A portion of starchy carbohydrates
- A thick slice of wholemeal bread (50g)
- Half a wholemeal bread roll, pitta, bagel or English muffin
- 1 medium baking potato, or the equivalent in smaller potatoes
- 3 rounded tablespoons cooked wholemeal pasta
- 2 tablespoons cooked brown rice
- 3 tablespoons (40g) low-sugar breakfast cereal
- 2 tablespoons no-sugar muesli.

A portion of fruit
- 2 small fruit (eg satsuma, plum, kiwi fruit)
- 1 medium fruit (eg apple, pear, banana)
- 1 slice of a large fruit (eg melon, pineapple)
- 1 cup of berries, grapes, cherries, etc
- 3 tablespoons canned fruit in juice or stewed fruit
- 1 tablespoon dried fruit (maximum once per day, as it's high in sugars).

A portion of vegetables
- Approximately 80g vegetables, or about 2 large tablespoons.
- A cereal bowl of salad
- One medium tomato (strictly speaking, a fruit).

(For a longer list of fruit and vegetable portion equivalents, see Chapter 3.)

Remember – potatoes count as starchy foods, not 'vegetables'.

Try to live by the '80/20' rule.
Eat healthily 80 per cent of the time, and you can relax for the other 20. Even better, adopt the '90/10' rule.

A portion of protein

(Try to make one or two of these oily fish, at least two beans and other pulses, and no more than two red meat, per week.)

- 100g meat or chicken
- 125–175g (or a small tin) fish
- 100–125g shellfish or prawns
- 1 large egg
- 4–5 tablespoons (or a small tin) beans or other pulses
- 2 tablespoons nuts or seeds
- 75–100g tofu.

A portion of dairy

(Although dairy products are good protein sources, they're given their own category here. Choose low-fat where possible.)

- 200ml (a medium glass) of skimmed or semi-skimmed milk
- 1 pot (150g) low-fat yoghurt
- 1 small pot (150g) low-fat cottage cheese
- 1 piece of cheese about the size of a matchbox (30–40g).

If you're dairy-intolerant or vegan, try to include calcium-enriched soya milk, yoghurt, etc, in your diet.

Fatty and sugary foods

These should be kept to a minimum.

Use low-fat or low-sugar alternatives where you can and save what you're allowed for the things you can't do without – perhaps a square or two of good quality chocolate, or a couple of biscuits a day. You can even splurge on a Danish pastry once in a while. You just need to keep your average on target by sticking to the healthy foods most of the time.

Go easy on the oil

When you need to fry something (for example, a stir fry) or for brushing roast potatoes or a piece of fish to grill, or for tossing grilled Mediterranean vegetables, you don't need any more than 1 teaspoon.

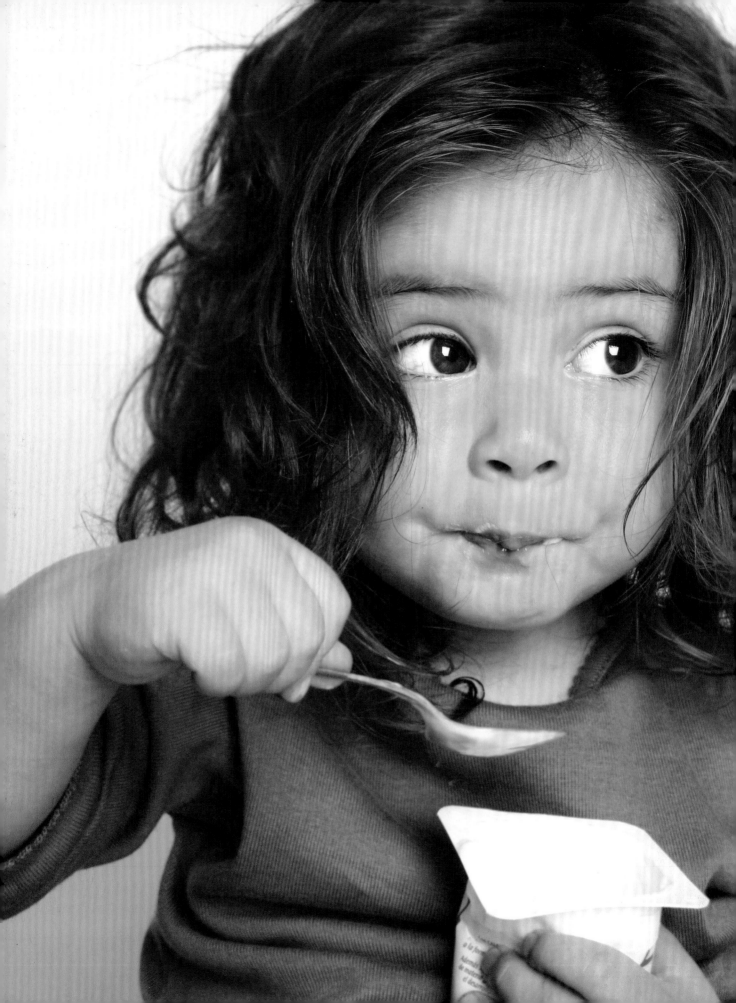

Chapter 2

The food we eat

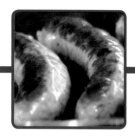

If you want to reap the benefits of eating healthily, you need to know a little about the nuts and bolts of nutrition. But when all is said and done, it's milk, meat, bread and soup you put in your supermarket trolley, not protein, carbohydrates and vitamins!

So, this chapter is going to be really practical. It will run through the main food groups, giving you the inside information on what they're good for, the best choices to make, and how to incorporate them into your diet.

The key to a good diet is balance. No one food or food group is 'better' or 'worse' than another (though highly refined carbohydrates have little to recommend them!). Moderation is the key – by eating a variety of healthy foods, you'll be able to hit all your nutrient targets. And what's more, you'll enjoy your food more – no one wants a rigid, limited and prescriptive diet.

1 Meat

Red meat

Red meat has had a bad press. It does tend to be high in saturated fat, and people who eat a lot of red (and especially processed) meat have a higher rate of certain cancers, including bowel cancer. On the other hand, red meat is a fantastic source of protein in a form that's easy for the body to use. It's also rich in iron, zinc and B vitamins.

Rather than avoid red meat entirely, think quality rather than quantity – it should be a nutritious treat rather than everyday fare. You can get the nutritional benefits of red meat while minimising the downside by choosing carefully and limiting your intake to, say, two or three times a week.

Some red meats are lower in fat and saturated fats than others.

	Total fat (%)	Saturated fat (%)
Venison	2.5	0.9
Pork	4	1.4
Beef	4.3	1.7
Lamb	8	3.5

Figures are for 100g raw weight

And the figures for processed meat products can be alarming.

	Total fat (%)	Saturated fat (%)
Salami	39.2	14.6
Pork pie	26	9.7
Beefburger (average)	25	10.7
Sausages (average)	25	7.9
Black pudding	21.5	8.5

Figures are for 100g raw weight

When buying and preparing meat:
- Minimise your intake of processed meat products
- Make your own burgers from low-fat mince
- If you must have sausages occasionally, buy low fat (look for 5–10% fat)
- Remove the visible fat from cuts of meat
- Grill steaks and chops with a marinade to keep them moist, rather than frying
- Bought mince often has a lot of fat 'minced in'. Buy inexpensive cuts of lean meat, and mince it yourself
- Venison is lower in fat than other red meats.

Bacon

Bacon is high in salt, and the curing and smoking processes produce chemicals that can increase our risk of cancer. If you love your bacon, buy unsmoked back, and keep it for an occasional treat.

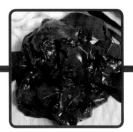

Offal

Don't dismiss offal – meats such as liver, kidney and heart. It's another great source of protein, and is rich in iron and zinc, along with vitamins A and D. What's more, it's full of flavour, quick to prepare and inexpensive.

Liver and vitamin A

Liver is such a rich source of vitamin A that if you eat it often, you could end up getting too much (once every couple of weeks is fine). Pregnant women are also advised not to eat liver, because too much vitamin A could harm the developing baby.

Poultry

Poultry is another good source of protein. It's not as rich in iron and zinc as red meat, but it's lower in fat, including unhealthy saturated fat. Choose 'real' poultry rather than processed, reformed and shaped products, which are likely to be higher in fat, and contain fillers and artificial additives.

With poultry you tend to get what you pay for. Intensively reared birds are likely to be higher in fat and have less flavour, not to mention the welfare issues involved.

Some types of poultry are lower in fat:

	Skin	Total fat (%)	Saturated fat (%)
Turkey breast	✗	0.8	0.3
Chicken breast	✗	1.1	0.3
Turkey dark meat	✗	2.5	0.8
Chicken dark meat	✗	2.5	0.8
Pheasant (roast)	✗	3.2	1.4
Duck breast	✗	6.5	2
Chicken breast	✔	13.8	9
Goose (roast)	✗	22	10
Duck breast	✔	42.7	10.7

Figures are for 100g raw weight

Fat-reducing tips

- Remove the skin from poultry – this is where most of the fat lurks. Grilled chicken breast is only 1.7 per cent fat, while the skin packs a whopping 40 per cent fat
- Dark meat (wings and legs) contains more fat than light (breast) meat
- Duck and goose are much fattier than other poultry
- In general, game birds such as pheasant and partridge are quite low in fat, though not as lean as chicken or turkey.

2 Fish

Few of us eat as much fish as we should – the Food Standards Agency recommends at least two portions a week, of which at least one should be oily fish.

Fish is high in protein, and rich in the minerals zinc and selenium (which support the immune system), and iodine (for the thyroid gland and healthy growth).

White fish

White fish include cod, haddock, plaice, coley, whiting, lemon sole, skate, halibut, Dover sole, flounder, hake, hoki, monkfish, pollack, mullet, snapper, sea bass, tilapia and turbot.

White fish is extremely low in fat, making it a great protein choice for weight loss and maintenance. It's also easy to digest, so good for invalids.

White fish, such as haddock, is a great protein source if you're watching your fat intake.

	Fat (g)	Saturated fat (g)
Lamb mince	13.3	6.2
Haddock	0.6	0.1

Figures are for 100g raw weight

Oily fish

Oily fish include salmon, trout, mackerel, pilchards, sardines, herring, kipper, eel, whitebait, tuna (fresh not tinned), swordfish, orange roughy and sprats.

While oily fish has a higher fat (and therefore calorie) content than white fish, it's the healthy polyunsaturated type that's good for our hearts and brains. Oily fish is also a great source of the fat-soluble vitamins A and D. Tinned oily fish where the bones are eaten, such as salmon, sardines and pilchards, contain calcium and phosphorus, needed for healthy bones and teeth.

The 'Eskimo Diet'

Why is it that the Inuit people of Greenland have such a low rate of heart disease, despite their high-fat, high-cholesterol diet? It's thought to be down to the omega-3 essential fatty acids (EFAs) (see Chapter 2) in their high-fish diet.

Other seafood, including shellfish

This group includes squid, crab, prawns, lobster, mussels, clams, cockles and scallops.

Their fat and omega-3 content varies – crab and mussels are quite good sources, but prawns contain hardly any. They're also good sources of the minerals zinc, selenium, iodine and copper.

Cooking fish

Fish is wonderfully quick to cook – one of the biggest mistakes people make is to overcook it, which dries it out and makes it tough.

The healthiest ways to cook fish are:
- Grilling
- Microwaving
- Steaming
- Baking in foil or greaseproof paper parcels
- Flash-frying in a pan wiped with olive oil.

Calories, fat and omega-3s in fish

	Calories (kcal)	Fat (g)	Omega-3 (g)
Oily fish			
Mackerel	239	13.9	2.6
Salmon	180	11	1.4
Tuna (fresh)	139	3.6	1.6
Trout	135	3.4	0.6
White fish			
Halibut	121	2.2	1.9
Plaice	92	1.5	0.2
Cod	96	0.7	0.3
Haddock	89	0.7	0.2
Other seafood			
Crab	128	5.5	0.4
Prawns	94	1	0.1
Lobster	103	0.8	0.2

Figures are for 100g raw weight

Fish and safety

Some people have been put off eating fish because of reports of toxins (particularly heavy metals such as mercury, and dioxins and polychlorinated biphenyls – PCBs) in their flesh. It's true that small amounts of these chemicals are found in fish, especially oily fish, and also sea bream, sea bass, turbot and halibut. Large fish (such as tuna) also have higher levels than small ones (such as sardines). But the medical consensus is that it's much better to carry on eating fish because of its health benefits than avoid it because of a small increase in health risk.

The recommended maximum intake of oily fish is up to two 140g portions of oily fish per week for girls or women who are pregnant or might have a baby in the future, and up to four portions per week for other women, and for men.

Pregnant women and young children should avoid eating swordfish, shark or marlin, and limit their intake of other oily fish (see Chapter 6).

3 Eggs

Eggs are about as near to a perfect protein food as you can get – after all, they provide everything a growing chicken needs! They contain more or less every nutrient needed by man (though unfortunately no vitamin C), and in forms easy for the body to absorb. Eggs have had some bad press, particularly due to their relatively high cholesterol content – this has now proven to be unfounded. There's no recommended maximum intake for eggs, unless a medical professional has advised you otherwise.

The cholesterol we get in our diet (from foods like eggs) makes hardly any difference to the important cholesterol numbers your doctor tests your blood for.

Nutrient content of a large egg

Nutrient	Whole egg	Egg white	Egg yolk
Calories (kcal)	75	17	59
Protein (g)	6.25	3.5	2.8
Total fats (g)	5	0	5
Saturated fats (g)	1.5	0	1.5
Monounsaturated fats (g)	1.9	0	1.9
Polyunsaturated fats (g)	0.7	0	0.7
Total carbohydrates (g)	0.6	0.3	0.3
Vitamin B1 (mg)	0.03	0.002	0.03
Vitamin B2 (mg)	0.25	0.15	0.1
Vitamin B3 (mg)	0.04	0.03	0.07
Vitamin B6 (mg)	0.07	0.001	0.0069
Folate (µg)	23.5	1	22.5
Vitamin B12 (µg)	0.5	0.07	0.43
Vitamin A (IU)	317	0	317
Vitamin E (mg)	0.7	0	0.7
Vitamin D (IU)	24.5	0	24.5
Calcium (mg)	25	2	23
Iron (mg)	0.72	0.01	0.71
Magnesium (mg)	5	4	1
Iodine (mg)	0.024	0.001	0.023
Zinc (mg)	0.55	0	0.55

IU, International Units

You'll notice that because egg whites are fat-free, they contain none of the fat-soluble vitamins A, D, E and K.

Eggs could also help with weight loss, probably because of their high protein content. A study from Louisiana State University in the USA gave overweight women breakfasts of either bagels or eggs. Each type of breakfast had the same weight and calorie count, but the women eating egg breakfasts felt fuller and more energetic, and consumed fewer calories through the rest of the day. What's more, they lost 65 per cent more weight than the bagel group, and their waist measurements shrunk by 83 per cent more.

And not only are eggs nutritious, they are also inexpensive, convenient, easy to store, and quick to cook in a variety of different ways.

Try these ideas:
- Spanish omelettes made with sliced cooked new potatoes and other vegetables of your choice such as peppers, spring onion, courgette or mushrooms
- Cheese and herb omelettes (add a small quantity of grated mature Cheddar cheese and a tablespoon of fresh parsley to the omelette halfway through the cooking time)
- Scrambled egg and smoked salmon on a toasted wholemeal English muffin. Or add some spring onions or sliced mushrooms to the scrambled egg instead of the salmon
- Poached egg and baked beans on wholemeal toast with grilled mushrooms or tomatoes
- Scrambled eggs on thick slices of brown toast. Add some spring onions or mushrooms and serve with grilled tomatoes
- Hard-boiled eggs sliced into wedges, drizzled with a tablespoon of low-fat mayonnaise on a large mixed salad. Add some sliced cooked new potatoes for a more substantial meal
- Make a pastry-less quiche. Make your favourite healthy quiche filling and bake in a lightly oiled individual baking tray.

4 Dairy foods

Dairy products, such as milk, yoghurt, fromage frais and cheese, are a great source of protein, vitamins (especially vitamins B1, B2 and B3 and folic acid) and minerals (especially calcium and phosphorus).

Just remember that much of the fat in dairy products is saturated, so it's best to choose semi-skimmed or skimmed milk, and other low-fat dairy products.

Three portions of dairy food provides most people with their full calcium requirement for the day (though children and young adults need slightly more), along with a good contribution towards their requirements for the B vitamins.

It's easy to incorporate three dairy portions into your day. A portion equals:
- 200ml skimmed or semi-skimmed milk
- 150g pot of low-fat yogurt
- 30g of cheese (small matchbox size)

These are just a few ideas to slip dairy into your diet:
- Skimmed or semi-skimmed milk on breakfast cereal or in porridge
- Low-fat natural yogurt or fromage frais added to naturally sweet fruit such as raspberries, mango or banana, topped with muesli, for breakfast or dessert
- A smoothie made from fresh fruit and yogurt, thinned with milk
- A low-fat yoghurt or fromage frais in a packed lunch, or as a dessert for dinner
- A piece of cheese in a packed lunch or as a snack
- Cottage cheese with oatcakes as a snack, or instead of sandwiches in your packed lunch.

Milk

Know your milk
Whole milk: 3.5 % fat or more
Semi-skimmed milk: 1.7 % fat
Skimmed milk: 0.1–0.3 % fat

Whole, semi or skimmed – which milk to choose?

Semi-skimmed milk is the most popular milk in the UK. Skimmed milk is virtually fat-free, and very low in calories. It's slightly better for calcium than other types of milk, but not so good for vitamin A.

■ For more calcium, fewer calories and less fat, go for skimmed milk.
■ For more vitamin A (but slightly more calories and fat) choose semi-skimmed.

Children under two years old should have full-fat milk, rather than semi-skimmed or skimmed, as they need the calories. If you want to move them onto lower-fat versions, wait until they are two years old for semi-skimmed milk, and five for skimmed.

Kinds of milk

Pasteurised milk has been heat treated to kill harmful bacteria.
Raw milk has not been pasteurised, and is generally only available from farms and farm shops.
Homogenised milk has been treated to break down the fat droplets in milk and distribute them through the liquid, so they don't form a layer of cream. Almost all of the milk we buy has been homogenised.
UHT (ultra heat treated) milk undergoes a higher heat treatment, has a longer shelf-life, and doesn't need to be refrigerated until it's opened (after which you should treat it as fresh milk).
Jersey and Guernsey milk is sometimes sold in supermarkets as 'breakfast milk'. It tends to

be slightly higher in fat and calories (and also vitamin A) thanks to its higher cream content.
Evaporated milk has been concentrated by approximately double, then tinned and sterilised. It can be skimmed, semi-skimmed or whole, and has a very long shelf-life.
Condensed milk is basically evaporated milk with added sugar. It can contain 60 per cent sugar, so should only be used as a very occasional treat.

Cream
Fat and calories in cream
Single cream:
   193kcal, 19.1g fat per 100ml
   29kcal, 2.9g fat per tablespoon
Crème fraiche (half fat):
   162kcal, 15g fat per 100g
   49kcal, 4.5g fat per tablespoon
Whipping cream:
   366kcal, 38.7g fat per 100ml
   114kcal, 12.1g fat per tablespoon
Crème fraiche (full fat):
   378kcal, 40g fat per 100g
   113kcal, 12g fat per tablespoon
Double cream:
   466kcal, 50.5g fat per 100ml
   149kcal, 16.1g fat per tablespoon
Clotted cream:
   586kcal, 63.5g fat per 100g
   176kcal, 19.1g fat per tablespoon

As you can see, cream, especially the thicker varieties, is alarmingly high in fat. If you need something to pour on your dessert, try low-fat natural yogurt (bio-yogurt tastes mild and creamiest) or low-fat natural fromage frais. For a thick spoonful on scones, instead of clotted cream, try Quark (a kind of low-fat soft cheese, at only 22kcal and 0.6g fat per tablespoon, a reassuring 16-times less than the cream alternative).

Yogurt
Yogurt is simply milk that has had a combination of harmless bacteria added in order to cause it to

ferment, thicken and gain its characteristic tangy taste.

Shop-bought yogurt can be high in sugar or artificial sweeteners and other additives, including artificial colourings. If you buy the yogurts with little portions of biscuits, crunchy muesli, or highly sweetened fruit puree, you can significantly increase the sugar and fat content too.

Types of yogurt

Set yogurt is made in the pot it's sold in, where it 'sets'.

Smooth/stirred yogurt is made in large vats, and stirred to create a smooth, thinner texture.

Live yogurt has harmless bacteria added to the milk during the production process that are still present and alive when it's sold.

Probiotic yogurts contain live probiotic 'friendly bacteria' that could be good for gut health.

Bio-yogurts are made using bifidobacteria and/or *Lactobacillus acidophilius*, which can also aid digestive health. It also has a milder, less acidic flavour than other yogurts.

The healthiest kind of yogurt is low-fat or virtually fat-free natural yogurt. If you're not used to its sharp taste, try these tips to incorporate this nutritious food into your diet.

Sweet ideas

- Add two tablespoons of yogurt to a bowl of porridge topped with chopped fresh fruit
- Stew apples with sultanas, swirl through some yogurt or fromage frais and drizzle with a little honey
- Make a sundae by layering yogurt, crushed digestive biscuit or muesli, and pureed fruit.

Fat and calories in yogurt
Full-fat yogurt: 119kcal, 4.5g fat per 150g pot
Low-fat yogurt: 84kcal, 1.5g fat per 150g pot
Virtually fat-free yogurt: 81kcal, 0.3g fat per 150g pot

- Turn out a set yogurt onto a plate, pour a moat of mango or raspberry puree around and serve with mango slices or fresh raspberries
- Mash blackberries, strawberries or blackberries and swirl into yogurt
- Fill pancakes with fresh berries, natural yogurt and a drizzle of honey. Roll up the pancakes and serve with berry puree
- Whizz with soft fruit and semi-skimmed milk to make fruit smoothies.

Savoury ideas

- Make yogurt salad dressings. Whisk together 2 tablespoons of natural yogurt, ½ tablespoon wine vinegar, ½ teaspoon mustard and a small crushed garlic clove or ½ tablespoon fresh parsley or mint
- Combine 3 tablespoons of yogurt with a tablespoon of low-fat mayonnaise and a tablespoon of chopped baby gherkins to make a sauce to accompany fish
- Combine 3 tablespoons of yogurt with a tablespoon of mayonnaise and a teaspoon of sweet chilli sauce to make a dip for homemade potato wedges or vegetable sticks
- Add finely chopped cucumber, a pinch of chilli and 1 teaspoon of chopped mint to a small pot of yogurt to make a quick sauce to serve with Indian dishes
- Mash potatoes with yogurt instead of butter and milk. Add flavour with a little mustard or horseradish
- Serve a small bowl of low-fat natural yogurt with chicken fajitas
- Marinate skinless chicken breasts in a marinade of 5 tablespoons of yogurt, the juice of half a lemon, and 1 tablespoon of medium curry paste. Bake or grill the chicken and serve with a large salad
- Make healthy hummus by whizzing a 400g can of drained, rinsed chickpeas, a clove of garlic, a 150g pot of low-fat natural yogurt, and the juice of ½ lemon in a blender until smooth. Serve with toasted pitta bread and vegetable sticks.

Fromage frais

This is a low-fat curd cheese similar to cottage cheese, but processed until it's smooth. Fromage frais is naturally low in fat, but some varieties have had cream added – you need to check the label.

Fromage frais can be used in the same way as natural yogurt. It has a milder, less sharp flavour.

Cheese

Cheese is concentrated milk. It takes about ten litres of milk to make one kilogram of cheese, so it's not surprising that it's a good source of the nutrients found in milk, such as protein and calcium. A small matchbox-sized piece of Cheddar cheese (30g) contains about 30 per cent of the recommended daily calcium intake for an adult.

However, cheese is also a concentrated source of saturated fat, and generally also salt. This makes it particularly important to choose your cheese wisely.

Different cheeses have different pros and cons. Once again, moderation is the key.

Choosing cheese

Hard cheeses (eg Cheddar, Lancashire, Wensleydale, Stilton, Gloucester, Danish blue, Edam, Parmesan):
- Higher in vitamins A, D and E than soft cheese
- But also higher in saturated fat
- Of the hard cheeses, Edam is one of the lowest in fat
- Parmesan has a very strong taste, so you only need to add a little bit to give a dish a cheesy flavour, cutting the fat content in the process.

Soft cheeses (eg Brie, Camembert, mozzarella, ricotta, mascarpone, cream cheese):
- Generally lower in saturated fat than hard cheese
- But also lower in vitamins A, D and E
- Cream cheese is almost as high in fat as most hard cheeses, so go for the low-fat versions
- Cheese spread (especially-low fat versions) is lower in fat than cream cheese. But beware added salt and other additives.

How much salt is there in cheese?

Too much salt can raise your blood pressure, so limit your intake of the saltiest cheeses, particularly if your blood pressure is already high.

Amount of salt in 100g cheese

	Salt (g)
Roquefort	4.18
Feta	3.60
Processed slices	3.48
Danish Blue	3.05
Edam	2.49
Gouda	2.31
Blue Stilton	1.97
Parmesan	1.89
Cheddar	1.81
Red Leicester	1.58
Double Gloucester	1.48
Brie	1.39
Cheshire/Wensleydale/Lancashire	1.25
Camembert	1.51
Cottage cheese	0.75

Fat-cutting tips for cheese fans

■ Recipes often call for far more cheese than is necessary. Try it with less – it may be fine, and you'll cut the fat, calorie and salt content drastically.

■ If you use the strongest, tastiest hard cheese, such as a mature Cheddar, you won't have to use so much in order to get a good cheesy taste.

■ Learn to love Parmesan – it's the strongest cheese of all, and a tiny amount goes an incredibly long way!

Cottage cheese

Cottage cheese is extremely low in fat (only 1.5g fat and 79kcal per 100g), and lower in salt than other cheeses.

■ Drain cottage cheese and use to fill split pitta breads with fresh salad vegetables or roasted peppers and mushrooms

■ Add a few snipped chives or a finely chopped spring onion and use to top crispbreads

- Add some chopped pineapple and pile onto toasted English muffins or ciabattas
- Drain tinned peach halves in juice and fill the centres with cottage cheese. A pair of peach halves with a large mixed salad makes a light lunch.

For variety, add one of these to natural cottage cheese:
- A couple of tablespoons of cooked diced chicken
- A slice of chopped lean cooked ham or turkey (roasted as a joint, not re-formed)
- Two tablespoons of cooked chopped prawns (defrosted if frozen)
- A tablespoon of chopped pineapple (you can use drained pineapple tinned in juice)
- Two tablespoons of finely chopped red and/or green pepper.

Dairy alternatives

Some people are intolerant to lactose (milk sugar), or allergic to the proteins in milk – but there are plenty of alternatives. Look for those that are fortified with vitamins and minerals, especially calcium, as non-dairy milks are naturally low in this vital mineral.

Try soya milk, rice milk, oat milk or 'nut milk' (eg almond milk). There's no reason why these delicious drinks can't be enjoyed by everyone, not just people who can't drink milk. They all taste different, and some are sweetened with fruit juice, so experiment until you find your favourite. Some non-dairy milks shouldn't be heated, as they may curdle.

Dairy products and weight loss

The calcium in low-fat dairy products could help you lose weight, and not just by saving calories. A recent Danish study found that low-fat dairy foods decreased the amount of fat people absorbed from their food. Calcium supplements didn't have the same effect – it had to be calcium from real dairy foods.

5 Grains, glorious grains

Grains are the seeds of cereal plants, such as wheat, rye, barley and oats, as well as less familiar varieties such as millet, buckwheat and quinoa.

Along with potatoes, grains are the staple starchy carbohydrates in our diets. All grains provide energy, but it's healthier to get your starchy carbohydrates from wholegrain, rather than refined, sources.

Wholegrains contain the whole goodness of the grain – the protein – and nutrient-rich 'germ' that would grow into a new plant, the fibre-rich bran outer layer, and the starchy layer that would provide energy for the growing seed. When grains are refined to make products such as white flour, the germ and the bran are stripped away – along with their nutrients and fibre content.

When choosing your carbohydrate foods, go for the wholegrain versions rather than 'white'. Choose wholemeal bread, brown pasta, wholewheat noodles, brown couscous and brown rice.

White flour in the UK has to be fortified with iron and calcium, and with the B vitamins thiamin and niacin. However, except for calcium, wholemeal flour is naturally richer in these nutrients, and it's also likely that the body finds it easier to absorb them in 'food form' than when they have been artificially added.

Nutrient content of white versus wholemeal flour

	White flour	Wholemeal flour
Protein (g/100g)	9.4	12.7
Fat (g/100g)	1.3	2.2
Carbohydrates (g/100g)	77.7	63.9
Fibre (g/100g)	3.1g	9
Calcium (mg/100g)	140	30
Iron (mg/100g)	2	3.9
Vitamin B1 (mg/100g)	0.31	0.47
Vitamin B3 (mg/100g)	1.7	5.7
Folic acid (mg/100g)	22	57
Vitamin E (mg/100g)	0.3	1.4
Potassium (mg/100g)	150	340
Zinc (mg/100g)	0.6	2.9

Benefits of wholegrains

- High in gut-healthy insoluble fibre, helping to prevent constipation
- Some kinds (especially oats) are rich in heart-healthy soluble fibre
- Low in fat (and the fat they do contain is the healthy unsaturated kind)
- A good source of many vitamins, especially the B vitamins and vitamin E
- Rich in minerals, such as antioxidant and immune-boosting selenium
- Contain phyto-oestrogens – plant versions of the female hormone oestrogen. These may act as oestrogen-boosters if your oestrogen level is low, and oestrogen-dampeners if your oestrogen level is high
- They are low glycaemic index (GI) foods, helping to keep blood sugar levels stable. (For more on the glycaemic index, see Chapter 7.)
- Their low GI also helps sustain you between meals, making it easier to lose weight or maintain a healthy weight
- Can reduce your risk of cancer, especially bowel cancer
- Can reduce your risk of cardiovascular disease (heart disease and stroke) by up to 30 per cent
- Can reduce your risk of type 2 diabetes by up to 30 per cent.

Wholegrains are great sources of:

- B vitamins (especially vitamins B_1, B_3 and folic acid)
- Vitamin E
- Iron
- Zinc
- Magnesium
- Selenium

Gluten

Some cereals (wheat, barley, rye and oats) contain the stretchy protein gluten, which is essential in the process of bread-rising. People suffering from gluten intolerance or coeliac disease must avoid any product containing gluten.

Choosing bread

When buying bread, look for wholemeal, with 2–3g fibre per slice. Seeds, nuts and kibbled grains add crunch, as well as extra nutrients.

White bread

This is flour that has been refined and the germ and bran are removed. It has to be fortified with calcium, iron and B vitamins by law. You can also buy white bread with added fibre.

Brown bread

Be aware that this isn't the same as wholemeal. It's made from refined flour, with varying amounts of fibre and germ removed, and sometimes colouring added to make it browner. It generally only has about half the fibre of wholemeal. Like white bread, it has to be fortified with calcium, iron and B vitamins.

Wholemeal bread

This is made from the whole grain, so you get the nutrition from the wheat germ and the grain's bran coat. It's fibre-rich, and doesn't need fortification as it contains vitamins and minerals naturally.

Granary bread

This can be made from any kind of flour, with added wholegrains. It's often made from wholemeal, but you'll need to check the fibre content on the packaging.

Multigrain bread

Depending on whether the 'basic bread' is made from white, brown or wholemeal flour, this can pack in the most fibre per slice with plenty of added nutrients – thanks to the added grains of various kinds.

Wheatgerm bread

This uses white or brown flour with at least 10 per cent added wheatgerm.

A study from Wake Forest University Medical School in the USA found that people eating 2.5 portions of wholegrains each day had a 21 per cent lower risk of cardiovascular disease than those who ate just 0.2 portions.

Know your grains

Barley: Try to choose pot barley rather than pearl barley, for maximum fibre. You can also buy barley flakes or kernels. Use it as an alternative to rice (cook in plenty of water for 45–60 minutes) or add to stews.

Buckwheat: Boil for about 5 minutes, and serve like rice. You can also buy buckwheat flour, buckwheat spaghetti, and soba noodles (made from buckwheat flour).

Gluten-free grains

Buckwheat, corn, millet and rice are gluten-free, so are suitable for people with coeliac disease.

Cornmeal: Also known as polenta, cornmeal can be cooked to form a paste and served like mashed potato. Or you can spread the paste into a dish and bake or grill it. Plain polenta can taste bland, so cook it in a tasty stock, or add herbs.

Millet: Sauté millet seeds in a little olive oil, then simmer in stock for 15–20 minutes, and serve like rice.

Quinoa: An ancient crop from South America, it's high in protein for a grain. Boil for 15 minutes until the round grains separate into 'spirals', and serve like rice.

Rice: Long-grain rice is generally used in savoury dishes, and short grain for rice pudding. Choose brown rice rather than white for maximum nutrients and fibre. Basmati rice has a lower (better) glycaemic index (GI) than white. You can also buy rice noodles and rice flour. Different types have different cooking times – check the packet.

Wheat: Generally used to make flour, but you can also buy wheat grains (wheat 'berries') to cook in water or stock for 40–60 minutes. These have a satisfying, chewy texture.

Bulgur wheat: This is par-boiled then cracked, so you only have to rehydrate it in boiling water or stock.

Semolina: This is a coarse, yellow wheat flour.

Couscous: This is made from little pellets of semolina grains. Rehydrate it in boiling stock.

Awesome oats

Oats are arguably the healthiest grain of all. They're a very low GI food, and are high in both insoluble and soluble fibre. The insoluble fibre helps your digestive system to function smoothly, while the soluble fibre lowers your cholesterol level.

Porridge forms the basis of a fantastic, low GI breakfast – make it with half-and-half water and skimmed milk to add calcium, and perhaps add a 'moat' of cold milk when you serve it. The Scots serve porridge the traditional way, with just a pinch of salt. But if you prefer a sweeter taste, rather than adding sugar, syrup or honey, try apple puree, mashed banana, or chopped fresh or dried fruit. Chopped nuts or seeds 'dry-roasted' in a pan can be added for crunch and extra nutrients.

Know your oats

Steel-cut oats: Whole oat grains cut into chunky slices. They have a chewy texture and take about 20 minutes to cook.

Rolled oats: Steamed and flattened between rollers. Less chewy than steel-cut oats and only take about 5 minutes to cook.

Porridge or quick-cook oats: Cut into smaller pieces before being rolled, so they cook in about a minute.

Instant oats: Precooked and milled so fine it only takes boiling water and sometimes a zap in the microwave to prepare them. But their GI is higher (ie not so healthy) as other oats. Also, they often have added sugar or sweeteners.

Breakfast cereals

Many people start the day with a bowl of cereal. There's no denying that it's quick and easy, and it can form the basis of a healthy breakfast, providing sustaining slow-release carbohydrates.

Many breakfast cereals are also fortified with vitamins and minerals – many children in particular get a significant proportion of their daily intake this way.

However, fortified cereals can still be unhealthily high in sugar and low in fibre, so do check the nutritional information on the packaging.

Good choices include:
- Plain shredded wheat
- Wholewheat bisks
- No-sugar no-salt muesli.

No-sugar no-salt muesli is very nutritious, thanks to the low-GI cereals, fruit and nuts. However, the fruit and nuts, although healthy, can bump up the calorie count, so keep an eye on portion sizes of 'luxury' mueslis if you're watching your weight.

Granola is high in sugar and fat – that's what sticks those crunchy little clusters together.

Watch out for the sugar content in cornflakes, bran flakes and bran sticks – they are often surprisingly high in sugar.

6 Sugar

In terms of nutrients, sugar doesn't have a lot going for it. It lacks protein, fibre and vitamins (brown sugar contains low levels of minerals, but not enough to be useful). It's high in energy, but the body prefers us to eat starchy carbohydrates which are slowly broken down into simple sugars, rather than the simpler sugars we're talking about here.

The problem is, humans are programmed to crave sweet tastes. Until comparatively recently, historically speaking, sugary foods were hard to come by and expensive, so even if we wanted sugar, most people had to do without. Now, we're surrounded by cheap and easily available sweetness. Our instincts still tell us to shovel in the sugar – and we do.

Most of us eat far too much of it – the recommended daily maximum is just 55g for a man and 47g for a woman, or about ten or nine teaspoons.

And that's not just the table sugar you add to your cereal or coffee – a lot of the sugar we eat comes from manufactured products. Many of these are obviously sweet – fizzy drinks are the main contributor to sugar in our diets, followed by sweets and chocolate, jams and other preserves, desserts, cakes and biscuits.

But there's also a significant amount hidden in processed foods that aren't particularly sweet, such as breakfast cereals (even the non-sugar-coated ones) and tinned fruit. You'll also find a surprising amount of sugar in savoury foods including tinned spaghetti, baked beans, tinned vegetables, pasta and other 'cook-in' sauces, tomato ketchup, brown sauce and other table sauces.

Too much sugar can lead to tooth decay and to weight gain, which predisposes us to conditions such as heart disease, certain cancers and type 2 diabetes.

Sugar can also crowd out healthier foods from the diet – people grab a biscuit as a snack rather than an orange, or drink cola or squash rather than water.

Table sugar is sucrose, but if you want to minimise the added sugar in your diet, it's not as simple as avoiding foods that contain this ingredient. You also need to learn the many names manufacturers use for sugars (many end in '-ose'), and look out for them on the labels. The nearer they are to the beginning of the ingredients list, the more the food contains.

Sugars on the labels:
- Sucrose
- Fructose
- Glucose
- Maltose
- Dextrose
- Lactose
- Treacle
- Honey
- Golden syrup
- Corn syrup
- Maple syrup
- Invert sugar
- Raw sugar
- Hydrolysed starch.

Good sugars

When we talk about sugar, we generally mean refined, table sugar, or sucrose. This is the kind of sugar we should limit in our diets. But some sugars can be good for us, thanks to the nutrients they're naturally 'packaged' with.

Many fresh foods contain natural sugars. For example, fruit contains fructose (fruit sugar), and milk contains lactose (milk sugar). But thanks to the fibre in fruit and the fats in milk, these sugars are less quickly absorbed and metabolised by the body, so they keep us full for longer. And the sugars in fruit also come packaged with vitamins, minerals and health-giving phytochemicals (plant chemicals), while milk is an excellent source of protein, calcium and fat-soluble vitamins.

Because of their other healthy benefits, these natural sugars aren't included in our recommended daily limit of nine or ten teaspoons of sugar.

Fruit juice

All this makes fresh fruit ideal for satisfying a sweet tooth, while boosting your nutrient intake. But what about pure fruit juice? It's high in vitamins, antioxidants and phytochemicals (beneficial plant chemicals), and you can count one 150ml glass of fruit juice towards your 'five-a-day' fruit and vegetable target. But because fruit juice has had the fibre removed and the sugars released, it's a high GI food, and causes a rapid blood sugar rise. It's also acidic, so it can damage your teeth. For this reason it's best to drink fruit juice with meals, or to dilute it half-and-half with water, especially for children. And check the label when buying fruit juice – you're after 100% pure with no added sugar or sweeteners, not 'fruit juice drink'.

Is honey healthier than sugar?

Honey, like table sugar, is mostly sucrose, and has virtually the same effect on blood sugar levels.

Teaspoon for teaspoon, honey is no less calorific than sugar, but it can help when losing weight. Because it tastes slightly sweeter, and has a distinct taste of its own (especially the darker honeys) you can often get away with using less – and this is where you can make calorie savings.

> Honey shouldn't be given to children younger than a year old because it can very occasionally contain bacteria that could cause a dangerous form of food poisoning in infants.

Cutting down on the sugar in your diet

In the supermarket:

- Learn to read the labels (see Chapter 10) and choose products with the lowest amount of sugar
- Look for the low-sugar options when buying sauces, baked beans and salad dressings
- Choose low-sugar or no added sugar cereals. Or make your own muesli with no added sugar
- Buy tinned fruit in juice rather than in syrup
- Instead of buying cartons of ready-made desserts, mash a banana, ripe pear or some fresh berry fruits and swirl them into low-fat natural yogurt
- Ditch the fizzy drinks and drink water or diluted pure fruit juice. Some cans of drink contain as much as thirteen teaspoons of sugar.

In the kitchen:

- Bake your own cakes and biscuits and reduce the sugar in the recipe. It will not adversely affect simple recipes, particularly if they are packed with dried fruit
- Use mangoes, berries and other soft fresh fruit whizzed in the blender to make sweet sauces or coulis
- For a quick snack (so you're not tempted to grab a chocolate bar) have a supply of sultanas, raisins, and chopped ready-to-eat dried fruits, almonds, Brazils, hazelnuts and walnuts handy
- Snack on fresh fruit, and base desserts around it. Provide a fruit bowl after lunch and dinner, or a fruit platter with different fruits cut into slices and chunks that everyone can share as a dessert. (This is the perfect chance to introduce new fruits to children.) Try kiwi fruit, apricots, melon, pineapple or mango. Serve the platter with individual small bowls of low-fat natural yogurt, drizzled with honey and topped with chopped nuts. Everyone can dip their fruit in their own bowl
- Use non-sugar or low-sugar toppings for crackers, rice cakes and in sandwiches. Try reduced-sugar peanut butter, pure fruit spreads, reduced-sugar jam, homemade hummus, low-fat cream cheese or yeast extract (use sparingly as it is high in salt).

7 Pulse power

Pulses are the protein-rich vegetables – beans and lentils. They also have a whole host of other nutritional benefits.

What's going for pulses

- High in protein
- High in fibre, both the insoluble and insoluble type
- High in starchy (low GI) carbohydrates
- Rich in vitamins, especially B vitamins, including folic acid
- Rich in minerals, especially calcium, iron and potassium
- Contain beneficial phytochemicals (plant chemicals)
- Low in fat – including the saturated fat found in animal protein.

If you follow a vegetarian diet, you should learn to love pulses. But they shouldn't be neglected by meat-eaters. Their low GI makes a pulse-based meal particularly suitable for diabetics,

Soya beans

Soya beans provide the highest quality protein of all the pulses. They also appear to reduce your risk of cardiovascular disease (heart attacks and stroke) thanks to phytochemicals called isoflavones.

You can also buy 'meat-replacement' products based on soya, and these can be a good way of varying the protein in anyone's diet, not just vegetarians. Try soya mince, soya chunks and soya burgers. Read the labels when buying processed foods as many are unacceptably high in fat and salt. In most cases, it would be healthier to buy 'plain' dried, chilled or frozen soya mince or chunks, and make your own meals such as stews, chilli, lasagne, or spaghetti Bolognese.

Tofu is bean curd, made from soya beans. It's high in protein, low in calories and fat, and although it's low in fibre (unlike 'whole' pulses) it's an excellent calcium source. 'Plain' tofu has little taste, but you can buy it marinated, or soak it yourself in a tasty marinade – it absorbs flavours like a sponge!

and anyone trying to keep their blood sugar in balance. They're also extremely filling, so they'll help you avoid temptation between meals, and are great for weight loss.

A diet high in pulses can also keep your digestive system functioning properly, thanks to the insoluble fibre, while the soluble fibre lowers your cholesterol levels and helps protect you from cardiovascular disease.

Using pulses

Dried pulses (with the exception of red lentils) need to be soaked overnight and cooked according to the instructions on the specific packets. But if that's too much hassle, many beans and pulses can be bought, ready cooked in tins. Try to buy them in water rather than brine (to reduce the salt content), but if this isn't possible, rinse them thoroughly.

Chick peas

Also known as garbanzos and chana dal. They can be used in soups and stews, and are the main ingredient in hummus and falafel.

Red lentils

Quick to cook, red lentils are popular in Indian

Quorn

Quorn is suitable for vegetarians (but not vegans, as it contains a small amount of egg white). It's not soya-based, but is made from so-called mycoprotein, which comes from a kind of fungus (a member of the mushroom family).

Quorn can be a convenient low-fat protein source and it contains fibre, too. It's available in many different forms, such as mince, chunks and 'fillets', which you can use in your own recipes instead of meat, as well as ready-meals, 'sausages', 'grills', burgers, and even vegetarian substitutes for sliced meats. But you need to check the labelling for salt, fat and additives, as the amounts can be high.

Bean tips

- Use beans or lentils to replace some of the meat in traditional casseroles, stews and curries. You'll slash the amount of saturated fat in the recipe, and boost the fibre, mineral and phytochemical content at the same time
- Make a tasty dip or sandwich spread by pureeing beans or lentils with a tiny bit of olive oil, perhaps a dash of lemon or lime juice, and seasoning to taste.

and Middle Eastern dishes. They cook down to a puree, and are excellent in soups.

Continental or green lentils

These hold their shape better than red lentils, and are often used as a 'bed' on which to serve baked fish or chicken.

Haricot beans

These are the beans in tinned baked beans.

Soya beans

These are used to make bean curd (tofu) and fermented to make soy sauce. They are also known as edamame beans, and you can buy them frozen.

Red kidney beans

A favourite in chillis and other Mexican dishes, they can also be used to make tasty veggie burgers and filling salads. Red kidney beans need careful cooking to destroy toxins present in the raw beans. Soak for at least eight hours, then drain and rinse. Place in a pan with fresh cold water to cover and bring to the boil, and continue boiling for ten minutes to destroy toxins. After this, simmer until soft (about 45–60 minutes). You can also buy red kidney beans in tins, which is much more convenient.

Black-eyed beans

Also known as cow peas, these are used in many dishes from the southern states of America.

Butter beans

These large white beans can be used to make burgers and added to stews and casseroles.

8 Nuts and seeds

Nuts and seeds are a great source of protein, heart-healthy unsaturated fats, and fibre. They're also rich in B vitamins, including folic acid, and vitamin E, as well as the minerals potassium, magnesium, calcium, iron and zinc.

Because different nuts and seeds contain different vitamins and minerals, try to eat a variety. These are the nutrients the different nuts and seeds are particularly good for:

Know your nuts

Almonds: Good source of healthy monounsaturated fats, vitamin E, B vitamins, zinc, iron, calcium, and magnesium.

Brazil nuts: Good source of protein and healthy polyunsaturated fats (one of the highest-fat nuts). A particularly rich source of the immune system-supporting mineral selenium.

Cashew nuts: Good source of protein, iron, potassium, and B vitamins (including folic acid).

Chestnuts: Good source of vitamin E and potassium. Not as rich in protein as other nuts, but higher in starch and lower in fat.

Hazelnuts: Good source of protein, fibre, vitamin E, magnesium, vitamin B1, and fibre. Relatively good for monounsaturated fats, but lower fat than most nuts.

Macadamia nuts: Good source of healthy monounsaturated fats – one of the highest-fat nuts.

Peanuts: Good source of protein (one of the highest protein nuts), vitamin D, fibre, magnesium, iron and zinc. (Actually a legume – a member of the bean family – rather than a true nut.)

Pecan nuts: Good source of monounsaturated fats and vitamin E.

Pistachio nuts: Good source of potassium, as well as monounsaturated fats, protein, magnesium and calcium.

Walnuts: Very good source of unsaturated fats (including omega-3 essential fatty acids) as well as protein, potassium, zinc, B vitamins (especially folic acid) and vitamin E.

Know your seeds

Flaxseeds: Also known as linseeds, these are a good source of fibre and omega-3 essential fatty acids (though these omega-3s are less easily used by the body than those found in fish oil).

Pine nuts: Very good source of protein, and contain polyunsaturated fats, magnesium, iron, zinc, potassium, and vitamin E.

Pumpkin seeds: Good source of zinc, protein, fibre, iron, magnesium, and potassium.

Sesame seeds: A particularly good source of calcium, also protein, polyunsaturated fats, zinc, iron, potassium and fibre.

Sunflower seeds: Good source of protein, polyunsaturated fats, iron, calcium, B vitamins, vitamin E and fibre.

> Nuts and seeds are rich in fats. Although these are the healthy fats we need in our diets, fats are still very calorie-dense (and nuts and seeds are very moreish!), so you have to watch your portion sizes.

Try these tips to incorporate more nuts and seeds into your diet:
- Keep a small pot of unsalted nuts and dried fruit (raisins, sultanas, blueberries, cranberries, apricots, prunes) in your desk and in the car for a quick snack.
- Sunflower and pumpkin seeds also make a quick snack.
- Add a tablespoon of finely ground nuts or seeds to fruit smoothies.
- Sprinkle seeds or chopped nuts on muesli or other breakfast cereals, or use as a topping for low-fat natural yogurt or fromage frais.
- Stir fry finely chopped celery and walnuts in a teaspoon of olive oil for two minutes. Serve as a crunchy accompaniment or sprinkle onto stews and casseroles just before serving.
- Make a quick sauce for pasta by stirring fresh pesto (made from pine nuts) into cooked pasta. Sprinkle over whole toasted pine nuts for extra crunch.
- Top white fish fillets with fresh pesto and grill.
- Add seeds or chopped nuts to sweet or savoury crumble toppings.
- Sprinkle toasted flaked almonds over green vegetables.
- Add toasted sesame seeds to stir fries.

Nutty energy bars

Grease a 17.5cm/7inch square baking tin and line the base with baking parchment. In a large bowl mix together a 225g/8oz can of crushed pineapple in juice, 2 tablespoons olive oil, 50g/2oz sultanas or raisins, the grated rind and juice of a small orange, 110g/4oz roasted seeds (sesame, sunflower, pumpkin and flaxseed), 25g/1oz chopped walnuts, 150g/5oz rolled oats. Spoon into the baking tin and bake at 200ºC/Gas 6 for 30 minutes until golden on top. Cut the mixture into fingers and leave in the tin to cool completely.

Buying nuts and seeds

Buy nuts and seeds unsalted. As well as the salt that can raise your blood pressure, salted nuts often contain added oil, and dry-roasted nuts generally have sugar and artificial additives too.

To stop them from going rancid because of their high oil content, nuts and seeds should be stored in a cool, dry place in airtight containers away from the light. The best place is the fridge or even the freezer.

9 Oils

We all need a moderate amount of healthy fats in our diets, and these generally come in the form of oils.

Different oils have different pros and cons, and some are better for certain uses – cooking, salads and so on – than others.

Know your oils

Olive oil: High in heart-healthy monounsaturates (though less good for omega-3s) as well as antioxidants that protect the body's cells from damage by free radical molecules. Good for salad dressings.

Sunflower oil: Fairly good for polyunsaturates (though mostly omega-6 rather than omega-3) and excellent for vitamin E. Very good for frying, as it's resistant to heat damage.

Flaxseed oil: The richest vegetable source of omega-3 essential fatty acids, so a good source of these nutrients for people who can't eat fish (the best source). It's unsuitable for cooking, as heat breaks down the omega-3s, but its mild taste makes it good for dressings where you don't want the oil to overpower other flavours.

Canola or rapeseed oil: One of the lowest in saturated fat, and rich in monounsaturates and polyunsaturates.

Corn oil: Rich in polyunsaturates, but not so good for monounsaturates. Good for frying.

Safflower oil: Low in saturates, and high in saturates. Suitable for frying.

Peanut oil: Rather high in saturated fats, but lower than butter and other animal fats. Suitable for frying.

Palm oil: Found in many processed foods, such as cakes and biscuits. Unlike most other oils, it's very high in saturated fats, so keep to a minimum.

Oils for cooking

Walnut, flaxseed and avocado oil aren't suitable for cooking, as heating breaks down their chemical structure, destroying their health benefits as well as their delicate taste. Use them instead to make tasty salad dressings.

Oils that can stand high temperatures, and can be used for cooking, include canola, sunflower and peanut. Olive and rapeseed oil are suitable for frying, providing you don't overheat them.

Sesame oil: Rich in vitamin E. Can be used for quick stir-frying (often used in oriental cooking). Strong nutty taste, delicious in a dressing drizzled over noodle salads.

Walnut oil: Contains mainly monounsaturates, as well as antioxidants. Another expensive oil, but its strong nutty taste means a little goes a long way. Great for dressings, but unsuitable for heating.

Pumpkin oil: Good for both mono- and polyunsaturates, and can be used for moderate heat cooking (such as roasted vegetables) though not frying. It's expensive, but its toasty flavour makes it great for dressings.

Avocado oil: Extremely rich in monounsaturates (though contains hardly any omega-3

Top dressings

Dress your salads with oil-free dressings, a tablespoon of reduced-fat mayonnaise or low-fat salad cream. Or make one of these simple dressings:
- 1 tablespoon lemon juice, 1 tablespoon vinegar, 2 tablespoons olive oil and 1 teaspoon of Dijon mustard
- 2 tablespoon low-fat natural yogurt, 1 teaspoon olive oil, and a teaspoon of chopped chives.

polyunsaturates) and also good for vitamin E. Good for salads and dressings. It can also be used for cooking (so long as it's not over-heated) though as it is expensive this is a bit of a waste.

Grapeseed oil: Good for mono- and polyunsaturates, and also rich in antioxidants. Has a neutral taste and can be used for frying.

Look after your oils
Oil rapidly oxidises and becomes rancid if exposed to air, light or heat.
- Buy cold-pressed oil if you can – many of the health-giving properties are lost when heat is used to extract the oil
- The healthier the oil, the more quickly it will go off
- Store oils in dark coloured bottles or in a cupboard, not in direct sunlight
- Buy in small quantities and use within a month or two
- Store in a cool place – oils spoil more quickly when exposed to warm temperatures, so they need to be refrigerated if you are not going to use them right away.

The fats in your fats and oils

Fat/oil	Main type	Saturates (%)	Monoun-saturates (%)	Polyun-saturates (%)
Olive oil	Monounsaturated	14	70	11
Rapeseed oil	Monounsaturated	7	60	30
Peanut oil	Monounsaturated	19	48	29
Walnut oil	Polyunsaturated	9	16	70
Wheatgerm oil	Polyunsaturated	19	17	60
Sesame oil	Polyunsaturated	15	37	43
Corn oil	Polyunsaturated	13	24	59
Soyabean oil	Polyunsaturated	14	23	57
Sunflower margarine	Polyunsaturated	16	20	41
Safflower oil	Polyunsaturated	10	13	72
Butter	Saturated	54	20	3
Lard	Saturated	39	45	11
Palm oil	Saturated	45	42	8
Vegetarian suet	Saturated	45	25	13
Suet	Saturated	50	30	2

Lard is classed as saturated, because it contains more than one-third saturated fat.

Choosing a spread

The choice of spreads available in the supermarkets can be daunting. It's impossible to find the perfect spread – they all have good and bad points. Here are the main things to look for:

■ Low-fat
■ 'Low in saturates' – check the nutritional information table for saturated fat content
■ 'High in monounsaturates'
■ 'High in polyunsaturates'
■ Olive oil (a monounsaturate) is a good ingredient to look for, but make sure it appears near the top of the ingredients list – otherwise it might be present only in tiny quantities.

■ Check the ingredients list for hydrogenated and partially hydrogenated fats and oils, and avoid them where possible. Look for 'low in' or 'no' trans or hydrogenated fats on the label.
■ Try a cholesterol-lowering spread – clinical trials have shown that they really do work.

Remember that even healthy oils are still liquid fat, with about 120 calories per tablespoon.

Olive oil

Olive oil appears to be one of the key ingredients in the super-healthy Mediterranean diet. It's high in monounsaturated fats, so lowers your level of harmful LDL-cholesterol without affecting your 'good' HDL-cholesterol, and reduces your risk of furred arteries, heart disease and stroke. It's also rich in antioxidants (especially extra virgin olive oil) which can protect us against the damaging free radicals involved in cardiovascular disease and cancer.

10 Fruit and vegetables

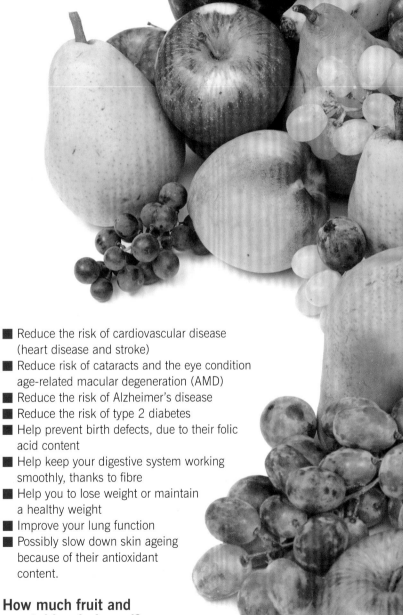

If you want to live longer and decrease your risk of the 'big killers' such as heart disease, cancer and stroke, eating more fruit and vegetables is probably the best change you can make to your diet. Not only could fruit and vegetables save your life, but they could also help protect you from a painful digestive problem called diverticulitis, and as you grow older, reduce your risk of cataracts and age-related macular degeneration, which can both lead to loss of vision and blindness. Fruit and vegetables may even help delay or prevent the onset of age-related memory loss, Alzheimer's disease and other dementias.

Fruit and vegetables are nutrient-dense. They're low in calories (provided you don't slather on the butter, oil or creamy sauces!), and full of vitamins, minerals, antioxidants, phytochemicals and both kinds of fibre (soluble and insoluble). This means they're great if you're trying to lose weight or maintain a healthy weight.

What's more, the nutrients in fruit and vegetables act together – they work in such a way that when you eat lots of *different* fruits and vegetables, the benefits aren't just added together, they're multiplied.

Fruit and vegetables are good for:
- Vitamins – they're particularly good for beta-carotene (which the body converts to vitamin A), vitamin C and the B vitamin folic acid
- Minerals – many are a great source of potassium
- Other phytochemicals including plant pigments. Many act as antioxidants and defend our bodies' cells from damage
- Natural sugars (especially from fruit)
- Fibre – both the soluble and insoluble kinds
- Water – we can get a significant amount of our fluid needs from fruit and vegetables.

Eating plenty of fruit and vegetables has been shown to:
- Reduce the risk of many cancers
- Reduce the risk of cardiovascular disease (heart disease and stroke)
- Reduce risk of cataracts and the eye condition age-related macular degeneration (AMD)
- Reduce the risk of Alzheimer's disease
- Reduce the risk of type 2 diabetes
- Help prevent birth defects, due to their folic acid content
- Help keep your digestive system working smoothly, thanks to fibre
- Help you to lose weight or maintain a healthy weight
- Improve your lung function
- Possibly slow down skin ageing because of their antioxidant content.

How much fruit and vegetables do I need?

It's recommended that we eat at least five portions of fruit and vegetables a day – but more is better. A serving equals 80g – that's one medium fruit such as an apple, small orange or peach, two small fruits such as satsumas, kiwi fruit or plums, half a grapefruit, a small bunch

Yellow: Pineapples, yellow peppers, sweetcorn
Green: Green grapes and apples, kiwi fruit, broccoli, peas, courgettes
Blue: Blueberries, black grapes
Indigo (or black): Blackberries, blackcurrants, plums, prunes, aubergines
Violet (or purple): Figs, red cabbage
And also white: Cauliflower, onions, leeks, turnips, mushrooms.

Fresh, frozen or canned fruit and vegetables

Fruit and vegetables are at their most nutritious straight from the tree or from the ground. But it just isn't possible for many of us to grow more than a small proportion of the fruit and vegetables we eat, and the produce you see in the supermarket could have been harvested several weeks ago – its vitamin content will have deteriorated over time.

But when food is preserved by freezing or canning, the nutrient loss is stopped in its tracks. Frozen foods are flash-frozen soon after harvesting, so vitamin loss is negligible. Fruits and vegetables are boiled during canning, so much of their water-soluble B vitamins and vitamin C dissolves into the canning liquid. The canning liquid is often highly sugared or salted, which means that if you use the liquid (and the vitamins), you get the sugar or salt as well, and if you throw it away, you lose those vitamins.

But even canned fruit and vegetables are better than none at all, and may contain more nutrients than fresh produce that's old and wrinkled!

of grapes, a cup of berries, a cup of vegetables, or a small bowl of salad. You can also count one glass of fruit juice, one tablespoon of dried fruit and one small tin of baked beans towards your daily target. Potatoes don't count towards your five-a-day – they're classed as 'starchy foods'.

You'll find more detailed lists of what a fruit or vegetable portion equals later in this chapter.

Eat the rainbow

It's also best to aim for at least five **different** fruit and vegetables to get a good variety of nutrients and maximise your chance of hitting your target for them all. Also, research from Colorado State University, USA, found that people eating a wide variety of fruit and vegetables had less evidence of the chemical reactions in the body that promote heart disease and cancer than people eating equal quantities of fruit and vegetables but of the same kind.

Many of the beneficial phytochemicals in fruit and vegetables are plant pigments – the compounds that give fruit and vegetables their vivid colours. So a good way to achieve the best mix of nutrients (and a great way to encourage children) is to 'eat a rainbow'. For example:

Red: Cherries, strawberries, cranberries, tomatoes, red peppers, radishes
Orange: Oranges, apricots, peaches, mangoes, sweet potatoes, butternut squash

Fruit and vegetables for fibre
Much of the fibre, and often the nutrient content, is found in the skin or just beneath it. In fruit and vegetables where the skin can be eaten, wash it well (even if it's organic) and eat it skin and all.

11 Fruit

Top fruit
While all fruit are healthy, some pack a more powerful nutritional punch than others.

Apples and pears
Rich in pectin, a soluble fibre that helps lower cholesterol. Great for snacking, or chop onto your breakfast cereal.

Apricots
These are fantastic sources of beta-carotene, a carotenoid plant chemical that the body converts to vitamin A. They're also good for iron and folic acid. Dried apricots are a great snack to keep in an office drawer.

Avocados
These get most of their calories from fat (a hefty 300 calories per avocado), but these are the heart-healthy monounsaturated kind. They also contain B vitamins and zinc. Add them to salads and sandwiches.

Bananas
Bananas are a rich source of potassium, which helps regulate body fluids and blood pressure, therefore reducing your risk of heart attacks and stroke. They're great for snacking, and also good whizzed into smoothies.

Dark-coloured berries
Berries such as blueberries, blackberries and blackcurrants are high in plant pigments called anthocyanins, which have a powerful antioxidant effect, reducing our risk of heart disease, stroke and cancer. Eat as they are, serve with low-fat natural yogurt and pancakes, or add to smoothies for an attractive purple colour.

Red grapes
You may have read that wine, especially red, is good for you. Part of its health effects appear to be due to a phytochemical called resveratrol, which is found in grape skins, especially the darker ones.

Cranberries
These contain compounds that appear to help prevent and treat urinary tract infections by preventing the bacteria responsible from 'sticking' to the urinary tract wall. Try to buy cranberry juice, rather than highly sweetened squash or juice drink. Alternatively take cranberry capsules. Blueberries contain a similar compound, and have a slightly lesser effect.

Fruit versus juice?
Whole fruit wins hands down.
- A 200ml glass of apple juice contains 76 calories, while a whole apple has only 40 calories
- Juice slips down so easily and you don't feel you've had anything, so you're likely to want more. An apple is high in fibre, so it fills you up. It also takes longer to eat
- The sugars in fruit juice have been 'liberated', so cause a rapid spike in blood sugar, followed by a sharp fall (juice has a high glycaemic index or GI, see also Chapter 7). The sugars in fruit are 'locked in', so they take longer to absorb – they cause a slower, lower rise in blood sugar (fresh fruit has a lower GI).

Lemon and lime juice

Lemons and limes are only moderately good for vitamin C (the juice of a lemon contains about 4mg vitamin C, while the juice of an orange contains about 26mg). However, a splash of lemon or lime juice can add flavour to dishes, minimising the need for salt, and lemon juice sprinkled on cut apple, banana or avocados stops them from oxidising and turning black.

What's a portion?

1 medium apple
3 apricots (fresh or dried)
½ avocado
1 medium banana
1 handful, or 9–10 blackberries
2 handfuls, or 4 heaped tablespoons blackcurrants
2 handfuls, or 4 heaped tablespoons blueberries
14 cherries
2 clementines
2 fresh or dried figs
½ grapefruit
1 handful grapes
2 kiwi fruit
6–8 kumquats
2 mandarin oranges
2 × 2 inch slices of mango
2 inch slice of melon
1 nectarine
1 orange
5–6 passion fruit
1 peach
1 pear
2 rings of tinned, or a large slice of fresh pineapple
2 plums
6 canned or 3 dried prunes
1 tablespoon raisins, sultanas or other dried fruit
2 handfuls raspberries
2 satsumas
7 strawberries
2 small tangerines
3–4 tablespoons tinned fruit

Dried fruit

Like fresh fruit, dried fruit is a good source of fibre, vitamins and minerals.

- 50g ready-to-eat dried apricots contain 1.7mg iron (15% of the recommended daily intake for a man, and 12% for a woman)
- 50g dried figs contain 125mg calcium (18% of the recommended daily intake for a man or woman).

Dried fruit becomes a concentrated source of energy (calories) when its moisture is removed, as its natural fruit sugars are concentrated too. So, if you're snacking on dried fruit, watch the portion sizes. However, its high fibre content slows down the uptake of the sugars into the bloodstream, and this and its nutrient content makes dried fruit a much healthier snack than, say, sweets or chocolate.

Don't assume that dried fruit is simply fruit that's been dried – it often contains additives. Pale-coloured dried fruit is often treated with the preservative sulphur dioxide, so that it keeps its bright colour. Some people (especially asthmatics and those with other allergies) can be sensitive to this additive, so you should buy unsulphured or organic dried apricots, which are brown rather than bright orange.

Other fruit is generally dried with added sugar (notably cranberries and blueberries). 'Ready-to-eat' fruit that has been partially rehydrated can contain potassium sorbate to prevent mould from growing. This additive, however, is unlikely to cause any problems.

12 Vegetables

Vegetables are even more nutritious than fruit. Once again, you need to eat a variety (in particular a variety of colours) in order to get the best effect.

Top veg

All vegetables are good for us, but some are spectacularly high in nutrients.

Green leafy vegetables (eg spinach, kale and swiss chard)

These are packed with vitamin C, folic acid and carotenoids. Some of them are also good for potassium, calcium and iron. They're also rich in a phytochemical called lutein, which helps keep eyes healthy into old age.

Brassicas (the cabbage family, eg Brussels sprouts, broccoli, cabbage)

These are rich in carotenoids (including beta-carotene), vitamin C, and folic acid. They also contain compounds called glucosinolates, which may help prevent cancer. Tenderstem broccoli is the best source of glucosinolates.

Orange and yellow vegetables (eg sweet potatoes and carrots)

High in the antioxidant pigment beta-carotene. People who eat a lot of orange vegetables have a lower risk of cancers such as bowel, lung and other cancers. However, it doesn't seem to be simply the beta-carotene that's responsible, and it's possible that this compound is simply a marker for an as yet unidentified phytochemical that's found alongside it.

Tomatoes

Tomatoes are the best source of a phytochemical called lycopene. This compound is a powerful antioxidant, reducing your risk of atherosclerosis, heart disease and stroke, and also of cancer (particularly prostate cancer). They're also a good source of immune-boosting vitamin C.

Unusually for vegetables, tomatoes are more nutritious when cooked. Canned and pureed tomatoes are actually healthier than fresh ones, as cooking them during processing makes it easier for the body to use the beneficial compounds inside them. Also, adding a little olive oil (or another healthy oil) makes the lycopene easier for the body to absorb and use.

Garlic and onions

This relative of the onion contains phytochemicals (including one called alliin), which have been proven to reduce your risk of high cholesterol, heart disease and stroke. Population studies have also found that people who eat plenty of garlic are less likely to suffer from several kinds of cancer. Garlic is also rich in the immune-boosting nutrients vitamin C and selenium.

Onions also contain similar compounds to garlic, but their health benefits are less dramatic.

What's a portion?

5 spears asparagus
1/3 aubergine
3 tablespoons cooked or canned beans
2 handfuls beansprouts
2 beetroot
8 florets broccoli
8 Brussels sprouts
1/6 small cabbage
1 large carrot
8 florets cauliflower
3 sticks celery
1/2 large courgette
3 inch piece of cucumber
1 leek
1 cereal bowl of lettuce
14 button mushrooms
1 medium onion
1 parsnip
3 heaped tablespoons peas
1/2 sweet pepper
10 radishes
2 heaped tablespoons cooked, or a cereal bowl
  of raw spinach
8 spring onions
6 baby sweetcorn, or 3 tablespoons tinned corn
1 medium tomato
6 cherry tomatoes
2 plum tomatoes
1 tablespoon tomato puree

Potatoes

Although potatoes don't count towards our five-a-day, they're still highly nutritious vegetables.

Provided we don't deep fry them (as in chips or crisps), or smother them in fat-rich sauces, they're a valuable part of a varied diet.

Potatoes are:

■ Low in calories
■ Virtually fat-free
■ High in starchy carbohydrates
■ A good source of vitamins, minerals and
  fibre.

Getting children (or veg-hating adults) to eat vegetables

Sadly, vegetables are much less popular than fruit, especially with children. Unfortunately, many of the compounds that make vegetables less sweet and more bitter than fruit are phytochemicals with impressive potential to prevent chronic diseases such as cancer and heart disease, and are found nowhere else. For example, it's the sulphur compound that makes Brussels sprouts bitter (particularly to some people, whose genes make them 'supertasters' of this chemical) that's one of the reasons they are so good for us.

Getting children to eat their vegetables (especially their greens) can be a challenge. Although the ideal is for them to enjoy vegetables, you may need to employ a wide variety of strategies and even engage in a little stealth. It's surprisingly simple to sneak finely chopped, grated or pureed vegetables into pasta sauces, soups, mashed potato, stews and casseroles.

We can also get starchy carbohydrates from other foods such as bread, rice and pasta, but their additional nutrition credentials are nowhere near as impressive as the potato's.

Potatoes are good for:

Fibre: A serving of potatoes (with their skins) contains 2.6g of fibre, which is 14 per cent of our 18g daily recommendation, more than a bowl of bran flakes, and nearly the same as two slices of wholemeal bread.

Vitamin C: Just one serving of potatoes provides nearly half of our recommended daily amount of vitamin C. They're nowhere near as rich in the vitamin as many other vegetables and fruit, but because we generally eat them in larger portions, potatoes provide a large proportion of our vitamin C intake in the UK.

B vitamins: Potatoes are a good source of these vitamins, particularly vitamins B1 and B6, providing 11 per cent and 22 per cent of our daily recommended intake.

Potassium: A medium potato contains approximately 22 per cent of our daily potassium requirement, and more potassium than a banana, or a serving of spinach or broccoli.

You don't need to avoid potatoes if you're trying to lose weight. A 175g serving of potato contains just 100 calories. You don't need butter on your new potatoes – a tiny splash of healthy olive oil is far better. And instead of oily mayonnaise and buttery toppings on your jacket potato, choose baked beans, tuna and sweetcorn with low-fat natural yogurt, or cottage cheese instead.

Potatoes are often thought of as high GI foods, and they are higher than wholegrains. But you can turn them into a 'slow release fuel' by following these tips:

■ Leave them in their skins – this is where most of the fibre is. Eat your potatoes baked in their jackets, or as homemade baked oven chips or potato wedges with skins, or have boiled new potatoes in their skins
■ Add a tiny bit of olive oil to new potatoes or mash – oil slows down the digestion time. Or use an olive oil-based dressing to make a cold potato salad
■ Don't overcook them. Potatoes boiled to mush or baked to powderiness are practically digested already, so it takes your digestive system no time at all to convert them to a blood sugar rise.

Chips

Not all chips are unhealthy. Homemade healthy chips (see box), and even some bought oven-chips – particularly with their skins on (check the label) – are low in fat and high in fibre.

The chips you need to beware of – the greasy culprits that have given them all a bad reputation – are:

■ Chips with crispy coating or flavourings – they'll generally contain hydrogenated and trans fats, plus artificial additives and a lot of salt
■ French fries from fast food restaurants – because they're thin cut, they soak up more oil
■ Chips from the chip shop – often greasy and fried in hydrogenated vegetable fat.

Crisps

Crisps should be eaten only occasionally. 'Regular' crisps contain about 34 per cent fat, or 8.3g per small packet. Even 'low-fat' or 'reduced-fat' crisps are about 22 per cent fat, or 5.5g fat per packet, so they're not really a low-fat food. If you must have crisps, go for baked crisps, which generally contain about 10 per cent fat, or 2.5g per packet.

Homemade healthy oven chips:

2 large potatoes, skins on
Pinch of salt
1 tablespoon olive oil
Freshly ground black pepper

Preheat the oven to 200°C/Gas 6. Wash the potatoes, cut into thick chips, leaving the skins on. Boil for 3 minutes then drain and cool under cold water. Place the oil in a large bowl, add the drained chips and toss to lightly coat them in the oil. Sprinkle with black pepper. Lay the chips on a non-stick baking tray or a piece of non-stick baking paper, bake for 30–35 minutes until they are cooked and golden. Turn a couple of times during cooking so that the chips brown evenly. If they brown too quickly turn the oven heat down a little.

The spices of life

It's worth incorporating herbs and spices into your dietary repertoire. Not only do they liven up the taste of your food, but many of them also have special health benefits.

Curry spices have especially impressive nutritional credentials.

■ A compound called curcumin, found in the yellow spice turmeric, could help prevent age-related mental decline and reduce the risk of Alzheimer's disease
■ Chillies contain a compound called capsaicin that makes them 'hot'. It has an anti-inflammatory effect when applied as a cream – scientists are looking into whether chillies in the diet have a similar effect
■ Ginger can be effective against nausea
■ Cinnamon could help balance your blood sugar and reduce blood pressure
■ Many curry spices, such as turmeric, cumin and paprika (as well as thyme and oregano), are high in salicylic acid, the active ingredient in aspirin. Scientists speculate that they could help relieve headaches. Salicylic acid also appears to reduce the risk of bowel cancer.

But this isn't an excuse to overindulge in oily curries – use these spices in low-fat Asian dishes, or to spice up a vegetable-rich chilli.

12 Water

Water is an essential nutrient. We can survive without food for weeks, but would die without water within days, or hours in hot conditions. Water isn't a fuel, but needed for every process in the body – including digesting and metabolising our food. It's also used for cooling the body (via sweat), and removing waste products (in urine).

Our body weight is approximately two-thirds water, and losing only one or two per cent of this can leave us feeling tired and woozy, sap our energy levels and cause headaches. We need about 1.2–1.5 litres (2.1–2.6 pints) of water a day, or about six to eight glasses (children need about six to eight small glasses). Not all of this has to come from pure water. Even tea and coffee count towards your fluid requirements, despite their diuretic effect, which is cancelled out by the water they contain. Strictly speaking, fizzy drinks 'count' towards your fluid intake, but since they have little else to recommend them nutritionally, aren't to be recommended. And don't even think of counting alcohol towards your fluid requirements!

Water-containing foods, especially fruit and vegetables, also contribute towards our fluid needs. However, it's a good idea to aim for 1.2–1.5 litres of pure water in order to keep well hydrated.

You should drink more water if you are:

- In a hot environment, indoors or out
- In an aeroplane
- Suffering from a fever, diarrhoea or vomiting
- Exercising strenuously.

People are notoriously bad at ignoring the need to drink. If we wait until we're thirsty, we could be well on the way to dehydration. Children and the elderly are particularly poor at judging thirst, so remind them to keep their fluid levels topped up.

It's better to drink little and often than huge quantities all at once. And drinking vast quantities of water can dilute the levels of salts in your blood, with dangerous results.

Other drinks

They may be less hydrating than pure water, but other drinks have their own nutritional benefits.

Milk: This is more of a snack than a drink, and is rich in protein and calcium. Go for semi-skimmed, or skimmed if you're trying to lose weight.

Fruit juice: A good source of vitamins, antioxidants and other phytochemicals, but also high in sugar and lacks the fibre found in the whole fruit. When you buy juice, make sure it's pure and not 'juice drink', which can be high in sugar and additives. And limit juice to about a glass per day, preferably diluted with water.

Tea: Contains healthy flavonoids, which can help reduce our risk of heart disease, stroke and cancer, and may reduce the risk of type 2 diabetes and slow down the ageing process. However, tea also contains caffeine and tannins, which hinder the absorption of nutrients from our food, so avoid tea late at night if the caffeine keeps you awake and drink it between meals rather than with them.

Herbal and fruit teas: Caffeine-free and can be drunk hot or cold. Many are reputed to have health benefits, particularly for relaxing. They can be a bit of an acquired taste – if you're new to them, start with a fruit tea, or camomile or peppermint.

Coffee: If it doesn't make you 'twitchy', or irritate your stomach, and you're not pregnant, there's no reason why you shouldn't enjoy a few cups of coffee (up to four) a day. It makes us feel alert, and could decrease the risk of some neurological diseases such as Parkinson's. But it's also our main source of the stimulant caffeine, so avoid it in the evening, and earlier if you're particularly sensitive to its effects.

Superdrinks

If any drink should be given the label 'super' it should be water, although tea and wine certainly have nutritional benefits.

Sports drinks

You don't need specialist sports drinks unless you're a serious athlete or doing an event such as a marathon. Otherwise, plain water is sufficient to hydrate you.
If you do feel you need specialised drinks, here's what the different kinds do:

- Isotonic drinks: Provide energy and fluid.
- Hypotonic drinks: Provide less energy than isotonic drinks, but more hydrating effect.
- Hypertonic drinks: Sugar-rich, to provide energy. Don't use during exercise, as they could actually cause dehydration.

Tea's health benefits

As well as the psychological feel-good factor of 'a nice cup of tea', the drink also contains health promoting antioxidants called flavonoids, and polyphenol chemicals called catechins.

These compounds can:

- Reduce your risk of heart disease and stroke by:
  - lowering blood pressure
  - lowering levels of 'bad' LDL-cholesterol
  - slightly thinning the blood and reducing the risk of dangerous blood clots
  - helping prevent damage to the artery linings that makes 'furring' and blockages more likely
- Reduce your risk of cancer
- Slow age-related mental decline, and even reduce your risk of Alzheimer's disease
- Possibly delay the signs of ageing

The 'best' kind of tea in terms of its polyphenol content appears to be white tea (a special variety, not 'regular' tea taken with milk) followed by green tea, but traditional black tea also contains plenty. However, it seems that when you add milk to black tea, it binds to some of the beneficial compounds, and their health-promoting effects are less evident. If you're used to drinking tea with milk, try it without, at least occasionally. You'll probably need to make it weaker at first, since the lack of milk can make black tea taste bitter, particularly if you're not used to it.

Tea also contains tannins, which hamper the uptake of nutrients including iron and calcium from the diet. Because of this, only drink tea between meals rather than with them, so that you absorb the maximum amount of nutrients from your food.

Green, white and redbush tea

White tea, and to a lesser extent green tea, have an extremely high catechin content, and you could also try Rooibos (redbush) tea, which is virtually caffeine free, and very high in catechins and polyphenols. It can be drunk black or white, and when taken black tastes less bitter than 'ordinary' tea.

Wine's health benefits

Wine is also high in polyphenols, especially one called resveratrol, so it has similar health protecting effects to tea. Red wine appears to work best, thanks to its higher resveratrol effect, but all wines and teas seem to have some beneficial effect. Just don't overindulge, as too much alcohol can have the opposite effect (see Chapter 4).

Chapter 3

Nutrition nasties

1 Salt

Too much salt can raise your blood pressure, increasing your risk of heart attacks and stroke.

The recommended maximum intake of salt in the UK is 6g per day, but the average salt intake is 10.2g per day for men and 7.6g for women. Fortunately, consumers are becoming more concerned about their salt intake, food labels are more comprehensive, and many food manufacturers are responding to pressure by cutting the salt in their products. The average intake is falling, but too slowly – it took six years to decrease by only 0.5g – and we still have a long way to go before we reach the target.

Unfortunately, most of us have grown up accustomed to salty food, so anything else can taste bland. But it is possible to re-train your taste buds surprisingly quickly. You can speed up the process by livening up your food with herbs, spices, and tasty ingredients such as lemon and lime juice. You should soon find that you appreciate the real taste of food, and that adding salt overwhelms the other tastes.

How much is safe for children?
Adults are advised to eat no more than 6g of salt per day, but because children are smaller than us they should have less. These are the recommended maximums, but less is better:

- 1 to 3 years – 2g salt a day (0.8g sodium)
- 4 to 6 years – 3g salt a day (1.2g sodium)
- 7 to 10 years – 5g salt a day (2g sodium)
- 11 and over – 6g salt a day (2.5g sodium).

Reading the label: Salt and sodium

Salt is sodium chloride. Because sodium is the harmful part, this is often what you'll see listed on food labels.

Here's how to calculate how much salt you're eating:

The amount of salt is the amount of sodium × 2.5. So a ready-meal that contains 1.3g of sodium per portion has 3.25g (ie 1.3g × 2.5) of salt per portion – which is more than half of your 6g daily maximum.

Also check that you're reading the amount per portion, rather than per 100g, as it can make a huge difference.

Salt savers

Research has shown that our palates quickly adjust to less salt in our food. Here are some simple ways to cut down:

In the supermarket:
- Always check the salt content of ready made products, such as soups, ready-meals and tinned food before buying
- Buy reduced-salt products when available
- Avoid processed meats such as burgers, sausages and re-formed meat – they're high in salt
- Limit your use of high-salt foods such as bacon, cheese, smoked fish, anchovies, olives or other foods in brine, stock cubes and gravies
- The amount of salt in bread on the supermarket shelves varies greatly. Check labels and choose those with the least salt, or make your own
- Use the varieties of cheese that are lowest in salt (see Chapter 4)

Salt myth

Over half of the people who buy rock salt believe it's healthier than other kinds of salt. But actually all types of salt contain the same amount of sodium – and it's this that may lead to high blood pressure if we eat too much.

- Cut down on ready-made cakes and biscuits. Make your own instead
- Before buying bottled and 'cook-in' sauces check a variety of brands to find the lowest salt content, as they can vary greatly
- Buy canned vegetables and pulses marked 'no added salt'
- Use a low-sodium salt in cooking, rather than 'ordinary' salt.

In the kitchen:
- Prepare as much of your food as you can from scratch using fresh ingredients
- When cooking, taste before you season and only add a little salt at a time, tasting each time. If your dish includes salty ingredients such as cheese, bacon, stock, soy sauce or Worcestershire sauce it may not need any salt, or only a very little
- When cooking vegetables add the salt to the water towards the end of cooking time, and you will need less
- Use garlic, onions, herbs and spices instead of salt to increase flavour
- Start the day with a bowl of porridge, or yogurt and fresh fruit, instead of reaching for the cereal packet. Many cereals are high in salt
- Swap salty snacks like crisps for healthy snacks such as fresh fruit or veggie sticks with a cottage cheese or yogurt dip
- Remove the salt cellar from the dining table – if it's not there you won't be tempted.

Try using garlic instead of salt to add flavour to some dishes.

2 Alcohol

In moderation, there's nothing wrong with alcohol, so long as it's just a glass of wine with a meal or the occasional social drink with friends. There's even evidence that particularly for certain groups of people (women after the menopause and men over 40 years old), moderate drinkers have a lower risk of heart attacks and strokes, as well as age-related mental decline, than teetotallers.

But drinking more than moderately can lead to:

- Alcoholism
- Liver damage
- Weight gain
- Increased risk of type 2 diabetes
- Increased risk of high blood pressure and heart disease
- Increased risk of cancers including liver, bowel, breast, oesophagus, mouth and larynx
- Stomach problems
- Sexual and fertility problems
- Serious risks to your baby if you drink during pregnancy or at the time of conception
- Increased risk of accidents (through intoxication).

Alcohol can also interact dangerously with prescribed drugs, disturb your sleep, contribute to depression and deplete your body of nutrients (especially the B vitamins).

How much is safe?
The official maximum safe intakes are:
- Women: 21 units of alcohol per week (no more than 2–3 units per day)
- Men: 28 units of alcohol per week (no more than 3–4 units per day).

Binge-drinking is particularly dangerous, so don't save up all your units for the weekend, and try to have at least a couple of alcohol-free days per week.

What is a unit?
There's a lot of confusion about what a unit equals. The Office for National Statistics has recently updated its definition to take into account the rising strength of alcoholic drinks and the increasingly large glasses used in pubs, clubs and restaurants. This recalibration meant that when the average UK consumption for 2005 was recalculated, it turned out to be 14.3 units a week, up from the 10.8 units we'd assumed previously.

When the units system was first devised, the glass used to measure a unit of wine was a **small** 125ml glass, not the large glasses holding 175ml or even 250ml that many pubs and restaurants now serve as standard – these can raise your tally to 1.5 or even 2 units per glass.

Also, when units were devised, wine was a standard strength of 8% alcohol by volume (abv). But today's wine can have up to 13% abv, making it possible to tot up 2.3 units from a glass of wine served in a modern 'standard' glass. You also need to watch the strength of beer, lager and cider – premium or vintage versions contain far more alcohol than 'standard' versions.

Remember too that an innocent-looking cocktail can conceal four or five units, and measures of spirits served at home or at parties tend to be more generous than pub measures.

Alcohol and weight gain

In order to maintain or lose weight, watch what you drink as well as what you eat. The body doesn't seem to register liquid calories very well, and drinks (even calorific ones) don't fill us up the way real food does, making it easy to put on weight without realising why.

Alcoholic drinks are also high in 'hidden calories'. A gram of alcohol contains seven calories. That's more than a gram of protein or carbohydrate – only fat has more. And sugars contained in alcoholic drinks increase the calorie count even more, so it's easy to pile on the pounds if you regularly knock back a few drinks.

Beers, lager and cider (per half pint)
Stout	105 calories
Bitter	90 calories
Pale ale	91 calories
Brown ale	80 calories
Lager (ordinary strength)	83 calories
Lager (premium)	169 calories
Dry cider	95 calories
Sweet cider	110 calories
Vintage cider	160 calories

Know your units

Drink	Volume (ml)	Strength (abv) (%)	Units
Normal beer, lager or cider			
Half pint	284	4	1
Large can/bottle	440	4.5	2
Strong beer, lager or cider			
Half pint	284	6.5	2
Large can/bottle	440	6.5	3
Wine			
Small glass	125	12.5	1.5
Medium glass	175	12.5	2
Large glass	250	12.5	3
Bottle	750	12.5	9
Spirits			
Measure/shot	25	40	1
Alcopops	275	5	1.5

Source: Office for National Statistics

Wine (medium 175ml glass)
Red wine	119 calories
Rose wine	125 calories
White wine (sweet)	165 calories
White wine (medium)	132 calories
White wine (dry)	116 calories
Sparkling white wine	133 calories

Fortified wine (50ml measure)
Port	79 calories
Sherry (dry)	58 calories

Spirits (25ml measure)
Vodka, gin, whisky, brandy, rum, etc	52 calories

Liqueurs (25ml measure)
Tia Maria, Drambuie, etc	65 calories
Cream liqueurs	81 calories

And don't forget the mixers – juice, cola and lemonade all add to the calorie count.

3 Additives

Food additives are nothing new – salting, pickling, and adding sugar to make preserves and jams goes back centuries. But while our ancestors used only salt, sugar, vinegar and other simple ingredients, modern food technologists have a huge range of chemicals available to them. Not all are added for our benefit, and some could be harmful if eaten in excess.

Additives are added to foods for many reasons:

- To improve the look and taste of food
- To keep food safe for consumption and increase its shelf-life
- To make food cheaper and easier to manufacture
- To make it 'healthier' (for example by artificially adding omega-3s or vitamins)

Additives as such aren't necessarily 'bad' – 'natural' substances, such as vitamin C, may be added to some foods as a preservative. And preservatives are responsible for preventing bacteria and fungi from growing in our food.

Even E numbers in themselves are nothing to be afraid of – they mean that the chemical has been tested and judged safe.

However, some people are concerned that the safe limits are not strict enough, and worry about the so-called 'chemical cocktail' effect: although the chemicals have been deemed safe in the doses normally consumed, there's little or no evidence about their effects in combination and over long periods of time – which is how in reality we eat them.

Also, some people (particularly children) are sensitive to certain additives. They may come up in a rash, or develop wheeziness or an upset stomach. There is also some evidence that some additives may affect mood or behaviour. This means that if there are any particular additives that you have found are a problem for you, you should always check the packaging when shopping.

Know your additives

Additives include:

- Colours
- Flavourings
- Preservatives
- Sweeteners
- Emulsifiers and stabilisers (stop foods from separating)
- Gelling agents and thickeners
- Humectants (keep foods moist).

Colourings

Colourings are added solely to make food look more appealing. When foods such as vegetables are processed they often turn an unattractive sludgy colour, so artificial colourings are added to return them to the colour we expect them to be. Colourings are also added to make food look more exciting – particularly sweets and desserts targeted at children.

Colourings must be the most 'unnecessary' additives, and some people (especially children) show behavioural symptoms when they eat certain artificial colourings. In-depth research has been carried out on several of these: Sunset yellow (E110), Quinoline yellow (E104), Carmoisine (E122), Allura Red (E129), Tartrazine (E102) and Ponceau 4R (E124), along with the preservative Sodium Benzoate (E211). The Food Standards Agency (FSA) has recommended that these additives are phased out of foods in the European Union, and as suggested that parents whose children show signs of hyperactivity might see an improvement if they remove the colourings from their children's diets.

Encouragingly, thanks to the backlash against chemical colours, many companies are switching to natural alternatives, such as E100, which is a yellow colour from turmeric. Beta-carotene, the pigment that makes carrots orange, is also used as a food additive. Check the ingredients list, or look for a 'no artificial colourings' flash on the packet.

Flavourings and flavour enhancers

You won't see any of the 4,500 permitted artificial flavourings named on the label – all you will see there is 'flavourings'.

These are often added to foods that are low in the 'real' ingredients that would provide flavour. For example, a strawberry ice cream that is low in real fruit needs artificial flavourings to make it taste fruity. It's far healthier to avoid these additives where possible, and eat food that gets its taste from natural ingredients.

Flavour enhancers don't contribute any flavour of their own, they simply bring out those already there. The most familiar flavour enhancer – E621 or monosodium glutamate (MSG) – has been found to cause symptoms including migraines, nausea and digestive problems, heart palpitations and asthma attacks in sensitive people.

Sweeteners

Artificial sweeteners contain only a fraction of the calories found in sugar, and most people associate them with 'diet food'. But they're also added to many non-diet foods, because they can be much cheaper than sugar, and like 'real' sugar, they are added to savoury as well as sweet foods. For this reason you'll also find them on the ingredients lists of many brands of tinned spaghetti and baked beans, sauces, dressings, pickles, crisps, dry-roasted nuts and other savoury snacks, as well as sweets, desserts, biscuits and baked goods.

Sweeteners are one of the most demonised additives, and although there is currently no scientific evidence that they pose a significant health risk (by increasing cancer risk, for example) they are another 'unnecessary' source of artificial chemicals in our diet.

Sweeteners also do nothing to blunt a sweet tooth, and may confuse our body's natural 'fullness' detection system. It's healthier to aim to gradually wean yourself off sweet tastes, choosing foods sweetened with just a little sugar, honey or fruit.

Know your sweeteners

Aspartame (E951) is probably the best known. You may also see it on the label as E951, Nutrasweet™, Canderel™, Equal™, Spoonful™, or 'contains a source of phenylalanine'.

Other artificial sweeteners include Saccharin (E954, or Sweet 'N' Low™, commonly used as a tabletop sweetener), Acesulfame K (E950), Sucralose (E955, or Splenda™).

Xylitol (E967) seems less contentious than other sweeteners. It also appears to have some health benefits, as it helps to prevent dental decay.

Preservatives

Without any form of preservation, food goes off very quickly, as moulds and bacteria flourish. Drying food, or adding salt, sugar or vinegar, were the original preserving methods (and are still used today). Later came bottling, tinning and freezing.

But most processed foods we buy today, unless they use one of the methods above, will contain some form of artificial preservative.

Some preservatives can cause adverse reactions in people sensitive to them. Those most likely to cause problems are:
- Sodium benzoate (E211)
- Other benzoates and parabens (E210–E219)
- Sulphides (E220–E228)
- Nitrates and nitrites (E249–E252).

Emulsifiers, stabilisers, gelling agents, thickeners and humectants are generally made from natural compounds and accepted as extremely safe. But the health implications of other additives remain controversial, and more research is now being carried out in this important area.

In the meantime, it seems sensible to do a bit of detective work, figure out whether any particular foods seem to cause you problems, and avoid them where possible. It's a good idea to start with those additives that seem particularly prone to cause problems.

The benefits of organic food

As well as the chemical additives incorporated into our diets by the food industry, there are also 'unintentional' additives in the form of pesticide residues that can remain on food crops, such as fruit, vegetables, and wheat and other cereal grains (such as those used to make flour).

The pesticide levels of crops and animal products are randomly checked to ensure they are below the levels set as safe. And it is extremely rare for food to exceed the safe limits. Because of this, we should still eat as much fresh foods such as fruit and vegetables as possible, whether or not we can afford to buy organic.

However, some people don't want to eat these chemicals in any amount, and are concerned about the 'chemical cocktail' effect.

Washing fruit and vegetables removes some residues, but not those that have soaked into the plant while it grew. Peeling removes surface pesticides, but also the vitamins that are concentrated just below the skin. And there's nothing you can do about the medications given routinely to animals to keep them healthy and help them to grow.

The most reliable (albeit more expensive) way to avoid pesticide residues is to buy organic.

What's different about organic food?

- Organic farmers are only allowed to use four out of the hundreds of available pesticides – and that's only as a last resort
- Organic foods aren't allowed to contain hydrogenated fat, the artificial sweetener aspartame or monosodium glutamate
- The use of other additives is minimised
- Genetically modified (GM) ingredients are not permitted
- Organic farmers don't use veterinary medicines on animals as a preventative measure. They can only use them when animals are actually ill, minimising the chance of these chemicals ending up in our food
- Although the research is inconclusive, some organic foods appear to be higher in nutrients. For example, organic chicken seems to contain lower levels of fat than non-organic chicken, and organic milk could contain higher levels of omega-3 essential fatty acids, vitamin E and the antioxidant beta-carotene
- Many people say organic food simply tastes better. Without artificial assistance from chemicals and drugs, food is allowed to grow and ripen, and animals allowed to mature, slowly and naturally
- As organic farming is less intensive than conventional farming, animals have more space, and welfare conditions may be better.

Cutting the chemicals

- Buy organic if and when you can afford it – to minimise your intake of pesticide residues and additives
- Grow your own – have organic vegetables and fruit at a fraction of the cost, and much fresher than produce from the supermarket
- Cook it yourself – minimise the artificial additives in your diet by minimising your intake of processed foods and eating home-cooked meals, made from wholesome ingredients such as lean meat and poultry, fish, healthy oils, pulses, whole grains, fruit and vegetables.

Organic 'junk food'

Organic food doesn't have to be good for you. You can still buy organic chocolate, biscuits, cakes and ready-meals. Although they avoid the chemicals mentioned earlier, they can still be unhealthily high in calories, fat, sugar and salt. It's just organically produced fat, sugar and salt!

4 Caffeine

The 'evil bean' has been demonised by many, but scientists now say that moderate intakes (say, three cups of 'real' coffee or five of instant per day) are fine for most of us, and may in fact reduce our risk of certain chronic diseases. So don't panic about your daily espresso, Americano or skinny latte.

You have to keep things in perspective. Caffeine is the world's most popular psychoactive substance – many of us can't get going in the morning without a cup of coffee! Caffeine makes us more alert, less tired, and some studies suggest that it can temporarily enhance some kinds of sporting performance.

But people who drink a lot of coffee can become dependent on it, and feel tired and sluggish when they're suffering from 'caffeine withdrawal'. Other people are so sensitive to caffeine's effects on their bodies that even a single espresso makes them feel twitchy.

If either of these is you, try to cut down on the caffeine by limiting your coffee to, say, one a day, or switching to decaffeinated coffee, tea (which contains less caffeine) or herbal teas.

Coffee pluses:
■ Increases alertness
■ Can improve exercise performance
■ Psychological 'feel-good' factor (we generally associate coffee with good experiences like taking a break)
■ Could reduce colon cancer risk
■ Could reduce liver disease risk
■ Could reduce risk of type 2 diabetes
■ Could reduce the risk of some brain-related conditions.

Coffee minuses:
■ Can cause anxiety/shakiness in sensitive individuals
■ Can disturb sleep
■ Reduces the amount of some minerals absorbed from food (so try to drink it separately from meals)
■ Can cause a short-lived increase in blood pressure (ask your doctor if this could be a problem for you)
■ High intakes can increase the risk of miscarriage and low-birth weight. Pregnant women shouldn't consume more than 200mg of caffeine per day.

The main source of caffeine is coffee, but it's also found in a variety of other foods and drinks.

Food or drink	Caffeine content (mg)
Espresso, Americano, etc	130
Cup of filter coffee	100
Mug of instant coffee	100
Can of energy drink	Up to 80
Cup of instant coffee	75
Cup of tea	50
Dark chocolate bar	60
Milk chocolate bar	25
Can of cola	Up to 60
Cup of hot chocolate	5
Cup of decaffeinated coffee	3
Cold cures/painkillers	Varies – check label

Chapter 4

Men and women, ages and stages

Although most of the nutritional guidelines hold true for everyone, men and women have some different nutritional requirements. Our needs also change through our lives and our lifestyles play an important role too.

For example, a growing toddler has different needs to a hungry teenager, and a man with a manual job will have different requirements to, say, a pregnant woman or an elderly person with a chronic illness.

1 Nutrition for men

Men are generally bigger than women and this, combined with their higher proportion of muscle to fat, means they need more calories (about 600 more than a woman per day), and more of the vitamins required for releasing energy from food.

Other nutrients that are particularly important for men include:

■ **Zinc:** Involved in male fertility. Get it from lean red meat, or seeds, especially pumpkin seeds
■ **Lycopene:** Could reduce the risk of cancers, especially prostate cancer. The best source is tomatoes.

The most recent National Diet and Nutrition Survey revealed that men are worse offenders when it comes to overindulging in foods high in saturated fat, and salt – both risk factors for cardiovascular disease. Also, although half of all men in a nationwide survey said heart problems would motivate them to lose weight, 37 per cent of these were a stone or more overweight, at least doubling their risk of cardiac arrest. So a heart-healthy diet and a sensible weight may be another area to watch.

2 Nutrition for women

It's not fair, but women's smaller size and lower proportion of calorie-burning muscle mass means that they can't consume as many calories as men without gaining weight.

These nutrients are of particular importance for women:

- **Calcium:** Women have a higher risk of osteoporosis, and this mineral is vital for bone formation
- **Vitamin D:** Needed to absorb calcium
- **Iron:** Women lose iron when they have their periods, and this must be replaced in order to prevent anaemia
- **Folic acid:** This is needed during a woman's reproductive years to reduce the risk of neural tube defects such as spina bifida in her baby.

Women who are planning a baby or who are pregnant or breast-feeding have very specific nutritional needs, and these are covered later in this chapter.

Being vegetarian

A vegetarian diet can be very healthy – or nutritionally dire. By avoiding animal products, you instantly remove one a major source of saturated fat. However, you also remove some fantastic sources of protein, iron, zinc and vitamin A.

If you're a vegan (and so additionally avoid eggs, dairy products and honey), you may also find it hard to get enough calcium and vitamin B12. For a list of vegetarian sources of these nutrients, and what they do, see Chapter 2.

A healthy vegetarian diet is based around wholegrain complex carbohydrates for energy. Pulses, nuts and seeds, along with low-fat dairy foods and eggs provide protein, while unsaturated oils provide healthy fats. There should be plenty of fruit and vegetables, too. A healthy vegetarian diet has plenty of variety, is low in fat (especially saturated fat) and salt, and high in fibre. And because it's based around plant products, a vegetarian diet is packed with health-promoting phytochemicals – literally, plant chemicals.

Several population studies have found vegetarians to have a reduced risk of chronic diseases such as cardiovascular disease, type 2 diabetes and cancer. But it's only the healthy eating vegetarians that see this benefit. Unfortunately, some people believe that vegetarianism is all about cheese and tomato pizza, chips, white bread sandwiches, sweets and chocolate, washed down with fizzy drinks.

Vegetarian watch points

Aside from making sure you get enough of the nutrients that can prove tricky for vegetarians, these are just a couple of watch points for veggies:

Easy on the cheese: Some vegetarians become overly reliant on cheese. It's a good source of protein and calcium, but high in fat, especially saturated fat, and also salt.

Help the iron: Iron from vegetarian sources is harder for the body to use than 'animal iron'. Eating vitamin C-rich foods at the same time helps your body to absorb more iron from your food.

Try these protein–vitamin C combinations:

- A glass of orange juice with a meal
- A vegetarian chilli with red peppers and tomatoes in the sauce
- A dessert of strawberries after a main course based around pulses and green vegetables.

3 Nutrition through the ages

Children

Childhood is one of the most important nutritional stages of your life. Children's bodies and brains must grow and develop, and what they eat impacts not only on their current health and wellbeing, but also on their health in the future. There's increasing evidence that adult susceptibility to disease is linked to nutrition in childhood and adolescence – early signs of 'adult' diseases, such as type 2 diabetes, high blood pressure and atherosclerosis (clogged arteries) are being seen in teenagers and even children.

Obesity in young people is increasing, and is linked with obesity in adulthood. Adult obesity in turn contributes to chronic health problems such as heart disease, stroke, type 2 diabetes and cancer.

Childhood is also a stage when we pick up food preferences and develop habits that may be very difficult to shift later on.

By feeding your children a healthy diet, you can give them the best possible start in life and set the stage for a long and healthy adulthood.

Pre-school children (age 3–4)

Because young children are growing rapidly and are generally extremely active, their requirements for energy (calories), protein for building healthy bodies, and the healthy fats, vitamins, minerals and phytochemicals needed for development, are extremely high for their size.

Key issue – Getting enough energy

For children this young, you don't have to exercise the same caution with full-fat foods as you do with older children and adults. Concentrate instead on the *kind* of fats they eat, and ensure that most comes from fish and foods containing healthy vegetable oils, rather than burgers, sausages, pizzas, chips and processed foods.

Because young children have small stomachs and short attention spans, it can be difficult to get all the nutrients they need inside them. Because they can't eat a lot at one sitting, they need small, tempting and highly nutritious meals.

Calorie requirements for children

Age (years)	4–6		7–10		11–14		15–18	
	Boys	Girls	Boys	Girls	Boys	Girls	Boys	Girls
Calorie requirement (kcal)	1,715	1,545	1,970	1,740	2,220	1,845	2,755	2,100

Remember that these recommendations are for an 'average' child.

It's also important to make sure that every calorie counts, and they're not filling up on nutrient-poor foods, such as sweets, fizzy drinks and crisps. Don't be tempted to use these foods as 'rewards'.

Some healthy foods can be too filling for pre-schoolers. High-fibre foods such as wholemeal bread, brown rice, wholemeal pasta can fill them up before they've eaten enough, so if your child says they're full before they have finished, swap them to the white versions until they're a little older.

Key issue – Food for growing brains

Not only are young children's bodies growing rapidly, but their brains are also developing at a speedy rate. This makes the omega-3 essential fatty acids (EFAs) that form such an important role in the brain all the more crucial at this stage. The best sources of omega-3s are oily fish (salmon, mackerel, sardines, and so on), although they should not have more than two portions per week. Flaxseed oil also provides omega-3s, but in a form that's less easy for the body to use. For more on omega-3s, see Chapter 2.

Research also suggests that trans fats could stop omega-3s from playing their proper role in building brain cells and membranes, so try to minimise your child's intake of processed foods (the main source of hydrogenated fats and therefore trans fats).

Key issue – Food for immunity

This is the age when children start school and come into contact with all those other children – and their germs! So you need to ensure they get enough of the nutrients that support their immune systems and help them fight off the bugs.

Vitamin A: As well as being important for immunity, this vitamin is also vital for the continuing development of the brain and nervous system.

Find it in: lean meat, oily fish, green and yellow vegetables.

Which milk for children?

Children younger than three years old really need the calories found in full-fat milk, but after this, they can switch to semi-skimmed. Fully skimmed milk isn't a good idea for children under five, as they need the calories found in semi-skimmed, which is also richer in the fat-soluble vitamins A and D.

Vitamin C: Another immune nutrient, also needed for wound healing (all those scraped knees!)

Find it in: Citrus fruits, strawberries, kiwi fruit.

Vitamin E: Helps vitamin C to work more effectively.

Find it in: Nuts and seeds, green vegetables.

Zinc: Needed for immunity and also for brain development.

Find it in: meat, dairy products, nuts and seeds.

Key issue – Acquiring new tastes
Early childhood is the best time to establish healthy eating habits, when children are at their most receptive to new tastes and experiences. But some children can be finicky eaters. This can unbalance their diets and set the stage for unhealthier eating in the future.

The secret is not to give up, to think laterally about different ways of presenting the food, and to be relaxed and not make a big issue of the fussiness.

Foods for children to avoid or minimise

- *Fizzy drinks:* Their sugars and acidity are bad for teeth
- *Shark, swordfish and marlin:* Children of all ages (as well as teenagers and women who could become pregnant) are also advised not to eat these fish because the low levels of mercury they contain can build up in the body. This rule is particularly important for young children, as the pollutants could affect a child's developing nervous system
- *Whole or coarsely chopped nuts:* They can cause choking, so shouldn't be given to children younger than five
- *Raw or partially cooked eggs:* To avoid the small risk of food poisoning
- *Fast food* and 'junk food' that's high in fat, salt or sugar
- *Sweets, chocolate, ice cream, cakes and biscuits:* High in sugar and often fat, so should only be an occasional treat
- *Crisps:* High in fat and salt. Baked crisps are lower in fat, but still high in salt.

Tips for picky eaters:
(These are applicable to children of all ages)

- Keep at it. Research suggests that children may have to be presented with a new food more than ten times before they will eat it. If your child doesn't like a new food, try again about a week later
- Introduce the 'one bite rule' – all you ask is that they try one bite
- If they don't like food served one way, try another. For example, if your child dislikes cooked carrots, try raw carrot sticks, or lightly cook them in a stir-fry
- Only introduce one new food at a time
- Don't prejudice their food choices with your own likes and dislikes. Just because you can't abide butter beans or olives, that's no reason why they should feel the same way
- Don't label your child as a 'finicky eater' or make a fuss about their refusing food. If they're doing it for attention, they'll soon realise they've achieved their aim. Instead praise them when they do try or eat a new food
- If your child refuses a meal don't be tempted to increase the size or number of snacks to fill the gap. If you stick to your guns the chances are they will be hungry at the next meal-time.

Juniors (age 5–9)

Just when children need to be eating really well to fuel their continued growth and help them to fulfil their potential at school, they start to rebel. Now children are making more of their own food choices, and this is also the age when peer pressure and advertising really start to exert their influence.

This makes it important for parents to continue to provide nutritious foods, discourage the less nutritious ones, and be a good role model for healthy eating.

Children this age are growing rapidly and need plenty of protein for building new cells. Make sure it comes from high-quality, low-fat protein, not fatty processed foods.

They're hopefully becoming more active, too, so they need increasing amounts of energy from wholegrain carbohydrates such as wholemeal bread, wholemeal pasta, brown rice and oats.

The immunity vitamins (vitamins A, C and E) as well as zinc, continue to be important, along with healthy unsaturated fats, all the other vitamins, minerals and phytochemicals that make up a balanced diet, and plenty of drinking water.

Key issue – Dental health

Now that children are getting their 'adult' teeth, dental health is particularly important.

Sugars are the main villain in tooth decay. Sugar provides food for the bacteria found in the sticky coating of plaque that forms on teeth. The plaque bacteria produce acid, which eats away at the teeth. Added sugars (rather than fruit sugars or milk sugars) are the most damaging. Milk, because it's rich in calcium and contains vitamin D (both important for healthy bones and teeth) is very tooth-friendly indeed.

When it comes to tooth decay, the frequency sugar is eaten is more important than the actual amount. After you eat a sugary snack, your teeth get an acid bath and it takes about half an hour for the acid levels in your mouth to return to normal. And each time sugar is eaten, the plaque bacteria get another meal, the acidity rises again, and the teeth take another hit.

Sugar-sweetened squash and fizzy drinks are particularly bad for teeth. And all fizzy drinks (including low-calorie, sugar-free or diet versions) are acidic, so they contribute to tooth erosion in their own right. Milk, on the other hand, is alkaline, and good for teeth.

The only drinks dentists recommended for between meals are milk and water. But if you find it difficult to persuade your child to drink enough fluids otherwise, well-diluted fruit juice or squash is lower in sugar and less acidic than pure fruit juice or carbonated drinks.

Say cheese

Research suggests that eating a small piece of hard cheese (such as Cheddar) after a meal or as a between-meals snack (to replace a sugary snack) could be a good way to help protect teeth from decay. Hard cheese is high in fat and salt, so watch the portion sizes.

Tweenagers (age 8–12)

At this age, you need to continue to ensure that children get their protein from healthy low-fat sources rather than processed food, that the vast majority of their fat intake is the healthy unsaturated kind, and that they concentrate on wholegrain carbohydrates, rather than white, refined carbohydrates, for energy.

Key issues – Iron and calcium

Iron

This mineral becomes increasingly important in this age group, for muscle growth (especially in boys) and to produce red blood cells.

Child-friendly sources include lean meat (make healthy burgers, meatballs, or Bolognese from low-fat mince), poultry and eggs.

Calcium

It's especially important for children and young adults to eat plenty of calcium-rich foods, along with the vitamin D required for calcium absorption, as these nutrients are needed to build and maintain healthy bones. This is especially important for girls and young women, as women have a higher risk of the bone-thinning disease osteoporosis in later life.

We only gain bone mass up until the age of about 30. Beyond that, bone is constantly being remodelled and replaced, but the rate of breakdown becomes faster than the rate of bone rebuilding. Calcium is gradually lost, increasing our risk of osteoporosis. This makes it particularly important to build up strong bones in the early part of life, to build up a good 'bone bank' to offset the later effects of ageing.

Child-friendly sources include low-fat dairy foods such as semi-skimmed milk, yogurts and fromage frais. Try to avoid those with added sugar or sweeteners, and liven up low-fat natural yogurt with fresh fruit, fruit puree or a tiny bit of honey.

Good calcium sources

Food	Serving size	Calcium content (mg)
Canned sardines (eaten with bones)	125g	518
Tofu	100g	510
Canned salmon (eaten with bones)	125g	300
Skimmed milk	200ml	244
Low-fat natural yogurt	150ml	243
Semi-skimmed milk	200ml	240
Cottage cheese	150g	191
Cheddar cheese	25g	185
Curly kale	80g	120
Baked beans	Small tin (200g)	117
Dried figs	40g	100
Sesame seeds	1 tablespoon (12g)	80

Calcium requirements at different ages

Age (years)	For boys/men (mg)	For girls/women (mg)
4–6	450	450
7–10	550	550
11–14	1,000	800
15–18	1,000	800
19+	700	700

Breast-feeding women need extra calcium (see section on breast-feeding)

Teenagers

Adolescents need a lot of food – it's a period of rapid growth and development, and their requirements for several nutrients are even higher than those of adults. Most teenagers have no trouble putting away enough food – the problem is with its nutritional value.

A recent national diet survey revealed that British teenagers ate too much sugar, salt and fat, and not enough fibre, fruit and vegetables. They were also deficient in several important vitamins and minerals.

Adolescents eat more fast food, sweets and chocolates than any other age group, and these foods are generally high in fat (especially the harmful saturated and trans fats) sugar and salt. They also tend to be high in calories, with the obvious implications for weight gain. Add the fact that portions of fast food and confectionary are generally large, and you can see that fast food and teenagers are a bit of an obesity time bomb.

We can't get away from the fact that teenagers

Alongside obesity, unhealthy obsessions with a perfect body are also seen in teenagers. A large proportion of teenage girls, and a few boys, are on or have been on slimming diets. While shedding excess pounds through a healthy eating and exercise plan is to be encouraged, unrealistic striving for skinniness can lead to eating disorders. Also, if teenagers ban or seriously limit food groups such as carbohydrates, meat or dairy products, they can lose out on fibre, a whole range of vitamins, plus iron, calcium, zinc and other minerals.

are almost adults – they have more choice over their food, and more of their meals are eaten away from home. The decisions are theirs, but parents also have what might be their last chance to help guide their offspring onto the nutritional straight and narrow, before they set off into the big, wide world.

Key nutrients for teenagers

Iron

Iron requirements are particularly high for adolescents. Teenage boys need even more than men, thanks to the rapid growth in muscle mass they're undergoing. Girls need still more because, once their periods start, they lose iron every month in the menstrual blood.

However, many teenagers don't eat enough iron. The average teenage iron intake is only 95 per cent of the recommendation for boys, and 62 per cent for girls. Iron deficiency and anaemia are common among teenagers – 20 per cent may be anaemic, causing symptoms such as fatigue, weakness and breathlessness during exercise, holding them back in school and everyday life.

It also matters where iron comes from. Because iron from animal products is much easier for our bodies to use than iron from non-meat sources, vegetarians may be more at risk from iron deficiency, and vegetarianism and veganism are common among teenagers – including up to 10 per cent of teenage girls.

Iron helpers and hinderers

Some foods aid the absorption of iron, and others hinder it.

■ Eating vitamin C-rich foods at the same time as iron-containing foods really boosts your iron uptake, so drink a glass of orange juice with your meal.

■ Tea and coffee contain tannins, which interfere with iron uptake. Save them for between-meal treats.

■ High-fibre diets, especially insoluble fibre such as bran, hinders iron absorption. But fibre is good for you, and vegetarian iron sources are high in fibre themselves. To maximise your iron absorption, just don't add extra fibre to your meals, for example by sprinkling wheat bran on them.

■ Spinach (even though it's rich in iron itself) and rhubarb, contain plant chemicals called oxalates, which also hinder iron absorption. Don't serve them with iron rich foods.

Good iron sources

Food	Serving size	Iron content (mg)
Liver	100g	17.0
Kidney	100g	6.4
Baked beans	Small tin (200g)	2.8
Lean red meat	100g	2.3
Dried apricots	40g	1.6
Egg	1 medium	1.3
Spring greens	2 tablespoons (80g cooked weight)	1.1
Nuts	30g	1.0

Iron requirements for different ages

Age (years)	For boys/men (mg iron)	For girls/women (mg iron)
4–6	6.1	6.1
7–10	8.7	8.7
11–14	11.3	14.8
15–18	11.3	14.8
19–50	8.7	14.8
50+	8.7	8.7

Omega-3 essential fatty acids

Because of their involvement in brain function, and their link with preventing depression, omega-3s could help make the turbulent emotions of the adolescent years more bearable.

Calcium

The rapid increase in bone mass during the teenage years means that teenagers need just as much calcium as adults, and boys need even more. Twenty-five per cent of peak bone mass is acquired during adolescence. However, the average teenager's calcium intake is 20 per cent lower than recommended. Vitamin D is also needed for calcium absorption.

Folic acid

Once girls reach reproductive age (so it's possible for them to become pregnant), folic acid becomes a key nutrient. This B vitamin plays an important role in lessening the risk of developmental defects in the foetus (see also Pre-conception and Pregnancy).

Adults – nutrition for special groups

Although the general nutritional information in this book holds true for most adults, some have special requirements.

Pre-conception

Both men and women should look to their diets before starting a family.

Three months (and preferably six months) before she intends to conceive, a woman should ensure she's fit, healthy and eating a nutritious diet – pregnancy puts a considerable strain on the body.

The crucial first stages of your baby's development take place before you even know you're pregnant, so you need to plan ahead so that you have sufficient reserves of the important vitamins and minerals to supply the embryo's requirements.

The right weight for a baby

If you're undernourished, you may find if difficult to conceive, and if you are severely underweight you may stop ovulating, and so certainly won't be able to become pregnant. Being overweight also decreases your chances of conception, as well as increasing the risk of pregnancy problems such as high blood pressure, gestational diabetes, and birth complications.

Nutrients you need

Zinc

Required for sex hormones, and for ovulation and fertility in women. Oysters are the supreme source (perhaps the reason behind their aphrodisiac reputation), but most people prefer getting the mineral from other shellfish, meat, fish, eggs, or nuts and seeds (especially pumpkin seeds).

Folic acid

Folic acid is required for the formation and development of the baby's nervous system (beginning between two and three weeks after conception) and a deficiency can increase the risk of a neural tube defect such as spina bifida.

Because this vitamin is so important during early pregnancy, all women are advised to take a supplement of 400μg (micrograms) from the time they start trying to conceive until the twelfth week of pregnancy. If you have already had a pregnancy affected by a neural tube defect, your doctor may prescribe a higher dose folic acid for you.

You should also eat plenty of folic acid-rich foods, including and green vegetables and brown rice.

Omega-3 and omega-6 essential fatty acids

Omega essential fatty acids (EFAs) are also vital for the formation of the brain and nervous system. Both omega-3 and omega-6 EFAs are important, but since omega-6s are much easier to get into your diet, women planning a baby should concentrate on getting plenty of omega-3s, from oily fish (no more than two portions per week), and from flaxseeds and their oil. For more on omega-3s and -6s, see Chapter 2.

Foods to avoid when planning a baby

Alcohol

Alcohol (and also drugs, both prescription and recreational) cross easily from your bloodstream to your baby's, putting the baby at risk from developmental problems, birth defects and premature birth. Heavy drinking during pregnancy can cause foetal alcohol syndrome – a collection of potentially fatal birth defects including low birth weight, retardation and heart defects.

A diet for would-be dads

A future father's diet is important too, in order to produce top-quality sperm. Sperm cells take about three months to mature, so men should get their diets in shape well in advance.

- Maintain a healthy weight – being overweight or underweight hampers your fertility
- Eat a nutritious diet based around wholefoods – to provide all the raw materials for healthy sperm
- Get plenty of zinc, from seafood, lean meat and seeds – deficiency leads to reduced fertility and low sperm counts
- Cut down on alcohol – it depletes your zinc levels
- Get enough selenium – another mineral needed for a good sperm count. The best source is Brazil nuts, but lean meat and seafood (also great for zinc) are good too.

Pregnant women are advised not to drink at all for the first three months of pregnancy, and no more than one or two units of alcohol a week after this. However, if at all possible, you should give up alcohol completely before you plan to conceive, because the foetus is at its most vulnerable during the first few weeks of pregnancy, before pregnancy has been confirmed.

Certain fish

Women who are planning a baby or pregnant should avoid eating shark, swordfish and marlin, because of the heavy metal pollutants that can build up in their flesh. Although the levels are tiny, they could harm a developing baby. For the same reason, you shouldn't eat more than one portion of fresh tuna or two tins each week if you're planning to conceive or are pregnant.

Vitamin A

This vitamin is essential for a healthy baby, but too much can harm its development. Therefore pregnant women and those planning a baby are advised not to eat liver (the richest source) or to take vitamin A supplements or cod liver oil supplements (also extremely high in the vitamin).

Pregnancy

Your food choices while pregnant are vital for your baby's development. You are now responsible for the developing foetus' every nutritional need, and the environment within the womb sets the stage for the baby's future health, lowering or increasing their risk of chronic diseases such as heart disease, stroke and cancer when they grow up.

Forget about eating for two in terms of quantity, only in quality – you have the two people's nutrient needs to consider now. You don't really don't need many extra calories – just an additional 200 calories a day during the last two trimesters of pregnancy. Make them count, by adding nutritious foods such as semi-skimmed milk, wholemeal toast, or a slightly larger portion of lean meat, poultry or fish. Adding some extra servings of fruit and vegetables is a good idea too.

To help provide for the developing baby's nutritional needs, a pregnant woman's body becomes super-efficient at absorbing nutrients from her food. It needs to be, because the baby comes first as far as its nutrition is concerned, and will 'steal' vitamins and minerals from its mother's body in order to supply its own requirements.

This is a vital protective mechanism for the baby, but it means that it's all too easy for a pregnant mum's nutrient stores to become run down if she doesn't eat healthily.

Key nutrients

Supplementary folic acid (for the first trimester) and plenty of omega-3 essential fatty acids continue to be vital.

Iron

Pregnant women can become anaemic (particularly if their iron stores were already low), as their bodies need to manufacture extra red blood cells (as much as 50 per cent extra) to carry oxygen around their body. In addition, the baby grabs a sizeable proportion of the iron its mother eats in order to make its own red blood cells.

The easiest iron sources for the body to use are animal products such as lean red meat and eggs. But don't overdo the red meat, despite its good iron content, as it's also high in saturated fat. And although liver is a supreme iron source, you should avoid it during pregnancy because of its high vitamin A content (see below).

You can also get iron (albeit in a form that's harder for the body to absorb) from vegetarian sources such as pulses, nuts, dried fruits, green vegetables and fortified breakfast cereals. Your doctor may also advise an iron supplement or a 'multi' supplement for pregnancy that will enhance your iron intake.

Calcium

The calcium to build a baby's bones comes entirely from its mother's diet, so it's important to eat enough calcium-rich foods to supply both your needs. Although calcium absorption from food becomes super-efficient during pregnancy, if you don't get enough, your baby will take calcium from your calcium stores in order to supply its own requirements.

Three portions of low-fat dairy products a day is an excellent way for pregnant mums to obtain calcium. Apart from dairy, other good sources include canned fish where the bones are eaten, such as salmon and sardines (also rich in omega-3s), sesame seeds and green vegetables (see also table under Tweenagers).

Vitamin D

You'll also need vitamin D to make the most of the calcium in your diet. Most people get enough from the action of sunlight on skin, but vitamin

> If you're having trouble meeting your nutrient needs during pregnancy, only take a supplement specifically designed for pregnancy, which won't contain an overly high level of vitamin A.

D is also found in oily fish, eggs, dairy products, and low-fat spreads that are fortified with the vitamin. Your doctor may also recommend that you take a supplement containing vitamin D.

Vitamin A
Vitamin A needs increase slightly in pregnancy, but too much can be harmful. Because of this pregnant women are advised not to eat liver and cod liver oil (the richest sources of vitamin A) or to take supplements containing vitamin A.

Fluid and fibre
Plenty of these help prevent the constipation that often plagues pregnancy.

Foods to avoid during pregnancy
Alcohol
Recent research suggests that even at lower alcohol intakes, drinking alcohol during pregnancy can be riskier to the unborn baby than previously thought, so it makes sense to avoid alcohol during pregnancy, or at least keep below the official recommendations of under one to two units of alcohol, no more than once or twice a week.

Caffeine
You don't have to completely avoid caffeine during pregnancy, but try to minimise your intake as high levels can lead to low birth weight and even miscarriage. Caffeine is also a sleep-disrupter, the last thing you need when you're probably already feeling tired.

Pregnant women are advised to consume no more than 200mg caffeine daily, the amount found in two mugs of instant coffee or four cups of tea. (See also table of caffeine in drinks and foods in Chapter 4.)

Food poisoning risks
These foods could give you food poisoning or harm your baby, and should be avoided:
- Unpasteurised milk
- Mould-ripened soft cheeses such as Brie and Camembert

> Ask your doctor or pharmacist before taking any medicines when you're pregnant or breast-feeding, even over-the-counter medicines, as they can cross over the placenta during pregnancy, or be passed on to the baby in breast milk.

- Blue-veined cheeses such as Stilton and Danish Blue (cottage cheese, cream cheese and hard cheese such as Cheddar are fine)
- Raw and lightly cooked eggs
- Undercooked meat or poultry
- Pâté.

Breast-feeding
A breast-feeding woman's nutritional needs are even higher than during pregnancy and she needs more calories and other nutrients.

Calcium
The most dramatic increase in need is for calcium – breast-feeding requires almost double the amount needed during pregnancy. Any shortfall will be made up by taking calcium from the mother's bones, so breast-feeding women are advised to include five (rather than three) servings of low-fat dairy products in their diet each day to ensure they hit their target.

Iron
Iron stores are generally severely depleted during pregnancy, so it's important to top up your stores. A deficiency can lead to anaemia, with symptoms of weakness and tiredness,

> You should avoid anything that could pass into your breast milk and harm your baby.
>
> - Avoid shark, swordfish and marlin
> - No more than two portions of oily fish a week
> - No more than 300mg caffeine a day
> - Avoid or minimise alcohol intake.

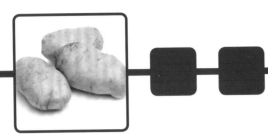

just when your new baby is demanding all your energy.

Omega-3 essential fatty acids
These brain-healthy fats are passed on to your baby through your milk when you're breast-feeding. Research suggests that babies born to mothers who eat plenty of omega-3s outstrip those of mothers who don't eat enough in terms of brain development. They were also less likely to show behaviour disorders such as attention-deficit hyperactivity disorder (ADHD) when they grew older.

Try to eat two portions of oily fish a week, but no more than this (see Pregnancy).

Protein
You'll also require extra protein, magnesium, zinc and vitamins A, C, D and folic acid.

Daily nutrient needs during breast-feeding

Nutrient	Breast-feeding requirement	Woman's usual requirement
Protein	56g for the first 4 months, then 53g	45g
Calcium	1,250mg	700mg
Magnesium	320mg	270mg
Zinc	13mg for the first 4 months, then 9.5mg	7mg
Vitamin A	950mg	600mg
Vitamin C	70mg	40mg
Vitamin D	No set recommendation	An extra 10µg
Folic acid	260µg	200µg

If you think you may not be hitting your targets through a healthy diet, ask your doctor or health visitor for advice on a supplement.

The menopause
The menopause is caused by falling levels of the female hormone oestrogen, which cause a decrease and loss of fertility, along with the other changes (both physical and emotional) associated with this life stage.

Some women sail through this phase, while for others it can be less easy. However, by eating healthily, concentrating on nutrients that are particularly important at this time, and avoiding any 'trigger foods' that give you trouble, you can help make the experience as smooth as possible.

Avoiding weight gain

As you grow older, your metabolism slows, and you can expect to gain 4.5kg (10lb) in weight between the ages of 20 and 60 – if you do nothing different. You can stave off this insidious weight change by keeping active, and appreciating that you may not need as many calories as you did when you were younger. Fill up on nutritious, nutrient-dense foods such as fruit and vegetables, rather than squandering your calories on junk food.

A healthy menopause diet

- **Slow-release carbohydrates** such as wholegrains and pulses to relieve energy dips and mood swings. Eating little and often will also help
- **Phyto-oestrogens**: literally oestrogen-like compounds from plants. Foods including soya products (eg tofu, miso and tempeh), seeds (especially flaxseeds) and celery. Research suggests that they could help relieve symptoms caused by fluctuating oestrogen levels
- **Potassium**: from nuts, sesame seeds and bananas. It can help banish bloating
- **Water**: ironically, drinking plenty of water also helps to prevent bloating.

It's also important to keep up your levels of calcium and vitamin D to help maintain your bones and prevent osteoporosis. A walk outside everyday provides weight-bearing exercise (the best kind for your bones) along with the sunlight needed for your body to produce its own vitamin D.

The elderly

It's hard to define 'elderly'. Most of us know someone who is sprightly and mentally sharp as a pin well into their eighties, nineties or beyond. But however young we may look and feel, there are some biological processes we can't deny, and our nutritional needs do change.

As we grow older, there is a natural tendency to lose muscle mass, and because muscle is our 'calorie-burning' tissue, this means our calorie requirements decrease. If we ate the same amount as when we were younger, we would put on weight – and this is what happens to many people. It is possible to slow or even halt this muscle decline, by keeping active and exercising, but often this isn't possible, and the only alternative to gaining weight is to eat fewer calories. This, in turn, makes it all the more important to eat nutrient-dense foods, and not squander calories on 'junk food'.

Other people find it difficult to maintain their weight as they grow older. Our taste buds become less sensitive, and loss of teeth, and chronic health problems may make eating a less attractive proposition. If this is true for you, or an elderly relative, you need to concentrate on small, frequent meals and snacks, that are packed with nutrients.

You can enrich the food of someone who has difficulty maintaining enough weight by adding dried milk powder to suitable dishes, to boost their protein and calcium intake. You can also provide extra calories by adding a spoonful of a healthy, neutral-tasting oil such as flaxseed or olive, to salad dressings, or a breakfast smoothie.

Key issue: Digestion

The digestive system of elderly people becomes less efficient. They are more prone to indigestion, and changes in the secretion of digestive juices and enzymes mean that nutrients are not so efficiently absorbed, which can lead to deficiencies.

Food also moves through the digestive system more slowly, making constipation a problem. Try to avoid it by eating fibre-rich foods such as fruit, vegetables and wholegrains, along with plenty of fluids.

Key issue: Dehydration

Unfortunately, elderly people often ***don't*** drink enough fluids, because their thirst mechanism doesn't work so well. Dehydration is a serious risk, making it particularly important to remind

older relatives to drink, and provide tempting alternatives if they don't like water, such as tea, herbal teas, or high-juice squash.

Key nutrients:

Omega-3 essential fatty acids
Once again, omega-3s are vital. They reduce the risk of heart attacks (which become more of a risk the older you get) and are also linked with better 'brain ageing', with less likelihood of age-related mental slow-down.

Calcium
Bone mass continues to break down faster than it is replaced, and as the years pass, the risk of osteoporosis increases. Help keep your bones strong by eating plenty of calcium-rich foods (see Chapter 2).

Vitamin D
This vitamin is needed alongside calcium for healthy bones, and unfortunately it's often deficient in the elderly. This is not least because, statistically speaking, they are less likely to be out and about in the sunshine, our main source of vitamin D.
People over 65 should take a supplement that contains at least 10 micrograms of vitamin D. You can also get it from oily fish, and fortified spreads.

Zinc
Immunity decreases with age, so 'immune nutrients' like zinc (and also selenium, and antioxidant vitamins) become particularly

important. A deficiency in zinc can dull the sense of taste, and correcting this is helpful in making eating a pleasure again.

Antioxidants
It's a good idea to keep up your intake of antioxidants (see Chapter 7) – they help maintain immunity, and reduce our risk of heart disease, strokes and cancer.

Lutein, zeaxanthin and beta-carotene
These plant pigments are important for eye health, decreasing our risk of an eye condition called age-related macular degeneration, as well as cataracts. The best sources are green leafy vegetables, maize, yellow peppers, carrots, and other yellow and orange fruits and vegetables.

Supplements

A multivitamin supplement designed for this life-stage, or a 'general' multivitamin providing at least 10 micrograms of vitamin D, is a good idea, in case absorbing enough nutrients from the diet is a problem. You don't need a 'mega-dose' supplement.

If you suffer from osteoarthritis, you may want to consider glucosamine and chondroitin supplements. They take a few months to work, and they don't help everyone – ask your doctor if you think they're worth trying.

Also remember to check with your doctor in case any supplements interact with any medications you may be taking.

Chapter 5

The effects of foods

1 Eating for energy

Eating healthily means plenty of energy, and not feeling hungry between meals. The secret is to choose filling foods that sustain you.

Our bodies need energy in the same way a fire needs fuel. Stoke it with the right raw materials and you'll have plenty of energy. Pile paper on the fire and the flames will roar for a short time and die down. Throw on some coal and the fire will burn slowly, for a long time. That's what you need for energy – a slow burn, from fuel that lasts a long time. Think of the sweets and biscuits as paper, and slow-release carbohydrates, such as wholemeal bread, brown rice or oats, as coal. So if it's constant energy you're after rather than the boom and bust provided by sugary snacks, your diet needs to be packed with starchy complex carbohydrates.

You also need food rich in vitamins and minerals to act as the matches to light the fire. Neatly enough, many of these micronutrients needed for metabolism are contained in slow-release, energy-rich foods.

The science of sugar

The body's ultimate fuel (and the only fuel useable by the brain) is the single-unit sugar, glucose.

The simpler a carbohydrate, the quicker it is for the body to break it down into glucose, for energy – it's easier to break down a simple sugar than a complex starchy carbohydrate.

Sugars are effective suppliers of energy, but this energy doesn't last long. When you eat a chocolate chip cookie, it's quickly broken down to simple sugars, which rush into your blood. But soon your blood sugar level falls, leaving you hungry again – and probably looking for some more cookies!

Although the body needs glucose for fuel, it's best not to supply it in neat sugar form. Far healthier is to provide a steady supply of energy, rather than a big burst that doesn't last. To achieve this, you want 'slow release' fuel, in the form of foods that take longer to break down, and therefore release their energy slowly.

Complex starchy carbohydrates are broken down slowly, so they provide a slow climb in blood sugar. This rise lasts for a long time compared with the spike followed by a crash you get when you eat simple carbohydrates, such as sugary foods and highly refined starchy carbohydrates.

In a nutshell, complex carbohydrates sustain you for longer, keeping you going between meals and helping you to keep your hand out of the biscuit tin at elevenses.

Glycaemic index and glycaemic load

The glycaemic index (GI) is all about the 'slow fuel' concept we described earlier. The GI describes the rise in blood sugar that a food creates, so foods with a high GI produce a sharp, rapid increase in blood sugar, while low-GI foods produce a smaller, more sustained effect.

The foods we want for slow, sustained energy are the low-GI ones. The GI also takes into account the fact that we generally eat foods as part of a meal rather than on their own. So, a low-GI food eaten with a high-GI food makes a medium-GI meal. This means that if you really want to enjoy a sweet treat, you should eat it with a 'slow release' low-GI food so that its effect on blood sugar levels is slowed and blunted. It's also better for your teeth to eat sugary foods as part of a meal rather than between them.

Cooking and processing also raises the GI of a food, so lightly cooked wholefoods are the best in terms of providing low-GI 'slow fuel'.

The glycaemic load (GL) is an extension of the GI way of eating that irons out one of the inconsistencies of the original concept. Several nutritious foods, such as carrots and watermelon, were given a high (ie 'bad') GI score, because they caused a large increase in blood sugar. But in order to experience that rise in blood sugar, you'd have to eat a huge amount of carrots, or a whole watermelon – far more than a portion. So, GL takes into account not only the effect of a food on blood sugar, but the amount of carbohydrate in it and how much someone's likely to eat at a sitting.

You can buy books full of GI and GL tables, but it's time-consuming having to look up every food you eat. Fortunately, you don't have to! You simply need to understand roughly how the whole GI and GL concept works, and common sense will tell you the foods to choose.

Here's the logic in a nutshell. It's a bit of a generalisation, but it'll get you by when you're in a hurry in the supermarket, or choosing between two options when you're eating out:

If a food:
- Is sugary
- Is highly processed and refined
- Is 'white' (as in white pasta, white bread, etc)

then it's likely to be high-GI, and therefore not a good idea to eat on its own.

If a food is:
- High in fibre
- 'Wholemeal' or brown
- Contains protein
- Contains fat (see below)
- Beans or lentils
- Vegetables
- Fruit

then it's likely to be lower GI, and is therefore fine to eat on its own – it won't send your blood sugar levels soaring. And, what's more, it'll also reduce the effect of any high-GI food you eat at the same time.

Fat is a bit of a double-edged sword as far as GI is concerned. Fat actually reduces the GI of a food. And while we try to aim for lowering the GI of our meals, we don't want to do it by piling on the fat.

So, you need to be sensible about fat and GI. By all means add a little splash of olive oil to white pasta if you haven't managed to persuade your family to eat brown yet – it'll make the meal more 'GI-friendly'. But don't use the 'fat is good for GI' argument to justify a meal of deep-fried battered fish followed by ice cream!

And remember, you don't have to demonise foods with a high GI – just treat them with care. It's not the GI of an individual food that matters as much as the GI of the whole meal or snack.

A high-GI food + a low-GI food = medium-GI meal.

The benefits of low GI

Eating the low-GI way isn't just good for your blood sugar and energy levels – it also benefits your overall health. A systematic review of studies on GI and disease risk found that low-GI diets reduced the risk of diabetes, coronary heart disease and gallbladder disease by up to 40 per cent.

Breakfast for energy

Most people know that breakfast is one of the most, if not *the* most, important meal of the day, but studies have found that one in four of us regularly give it a miss.

Skip breakfast, and by mid-morning you'll feel sluggish and irritable. A filling, nourishing breakfast sets you up for the day, kick-starting your metabolic rate, sustaining your energy levels through the morning, and giving you the self-control to resist the biscuits or doughnuts that seem so tempting mid-morning, but leave you craving more soon afterwards.

A lot of women still believe that skipping breakfast is a useful slimming strategy, but research shows that if you miss out on this vital meal you're generally more than make up for it calorie-wise during the day. You'll also find it harder to meet your daily nutrient requirements for the day.

What makes a good breakfast?

A good breakfast should provide slow-release wholegrain carbohydrate, some protein, and preferably some fruit for vitamin C and other vitamins, minerals and phytochemicals.

It's tempting to skip breakfast on weekdays when you're in a hurry, so here are some fast and nutritious ideas:

- Top two wholewheat bisks with a handful of blueberries and serve with semi-skimmed milk, 2 tablespoons natural yogurt, and a drizzle of honey if needed
- Spread a slice of wholemeal toast with low-fat cream cheese, a small sliced banana and a drizzle of honey if needed
- Fill a medium bowl with chopped fresh fruit and top with 2 tablespoons no-added-sugar/no-added-salt muesli and 3 tablespoons low-fat natural yogurt
- Have 2 slices of wholemeal toast spread with a little olive spread and reduced-sugar marmalade, and a piece of fresh fruit
- A slice of wholemeal bread topped with three tablespoons of baked beans. Plus a piece of fruit
- A fruit smoothie made with half a banana, half a mango, 3 tablespoons natural yogurt and 100ml skimmed or semi-skimmed milk.

You can be more adventurous when you have a little more time. Here are some 'weekend breakfasts':

- Three Scotch pancakes layered with low-fat natural yogurt, crushed mixed berries (any combination of raspberries, blueberries, blackberries or strawberries) and drizzled with a little honey if needed
- An English muffin (wholemeal if possible) or half a large multi-grain bagel toasted and topped with scrambled egg and smoked salmon
- A toasted English muffin topped with a poached egg, grilled tomatoes and mushrooms.

2 Food and immunity

*Our bodies are constantly under attack
– it's amazing that we're not constantly ill.
Thankfully, we have strong defences:*

■ **Our skin:** This includes both our 'outside skin', and the 'inside skin', or mucous membranes that line our mouth, nose, and digestive system. Together they form a germproof barrier against the outside world
■ **Immune system:** This battles germs that get through the first line of defence and into our bodies
■ **Antioxidant defences:** These help protect us from non-infectious diseases such as cancer and heart disease.

Unsurprisingly, our diet has a huge effect on our body's defences. Eat badly, and it will soon show in your skin's condition, and also its ability to provide a germ-proof barrier. Essential fatty acids and vitamins A and E are particularly important for this. A variety of nutrients have been shown to support the immune system, while certain foods are rich in antioxidants.

The immune system

Your immune system determines whether or not you catch a 'bug' or infection, and if you do, how long it takes you to shake it off. Good nutrition supports the immune system, enhancing our body's defences against bacteria and viruses and other so-called pathogens.

You can see this dramatically illustrated when a country is struck by a natural disaster such as famine. Disease often soon becomes a problem, and one of the reasons for this is because malnutrition has a devastating effect on the immune system's defences.

Poor nutrition can weaken our own immune systems. If we crash diet and don't eat enough calories or protein, we're more vulnerable to illness. Ironically, eating too much fat, and being obese, also hampers our body's defences.

All of these stop the immune system from functioning at its best:

■ Stress
■ Lack of exercise
■ Very-low-calorie diets (below about 1,200kcal per day)
■ Obesity
■ High-fat diet
■ Over-exercising
■ Lack of sleep
■ Cigarette smoke and pollution.

Immune boosters
Give your defences all the support you can with these nutrients.

Vitamin A
This protective vitamin is vital to keep our skin and the mucous membranes lining the nose, mouth, throat, digestive tract and lungs healthy, so that they provide an effective barrier against germs outside our body or those that get into our lungs or digestive system.

You can get your vitamin A as 'pre-formed' vitamin A (called retinol) from animal sources, such as meat. But the body can also make vitamin A from beta-carotene, which is found in orange and yellow fruit and vegetables. Remember that vitamin A is stored in the body, so it's possible for toxic levels to build up if your intake is too high over a long period of time. If you eat a normal, healthy diet, this shouldn't be a problem unless you eat a lot of liver (the richest source of vitamin A). However, some vitamin supplements can contain high doses of

this vitamin, which could tip you over into the danger zone. It's best to get moderate amounts of vitamin A from animal sources, and plenty of beta-carotene from plant sources, and let the body naturally regulate how much of this plant precursor is converted to the immune-fighting vitamin A. It's very unlikely that you'd be able to overdose on vitamin A by eating beta-carotene, because when the body has enough vitamin A, it stops making it. Also, carotenoids such as beta-carotene are also excellent antioxidants (see below) in their own right.

Vitamins C and E
These help support the immune system, and also work together as antioxidants. Getting enough vitamin C is also important for wound healing.

Zinc
Probably the most important defensive mineral, zinc boosts the immune system's infection-fighting T cells. People who are deficient in zinc are particularly vulnerable to infection.

Selenium
Although the mineral selenium is needed only in trace amounts, it's vital for the immune defences.

Bio-yogurt
Bio-yogurt may enhance immune defences in the gut. Research suggests that this could not only protect us from infections in the digestive system, but also from other illnesses, including the common cold.

3 Phytochemicals

'Phyto' is Greek for plant, so phytochemical literally means 'plant chemical'. These compounds are behind many of the healthy properties of fruit and vegetables. Some vitamins (those found in vegetarian sources) are phytochemicals, but there are plenty more, such as:

- The pigments that make cabbage green, tomatoes red, carrots orange and blueberries purple
- The chemicals that give raw Brussels sprouts their mouth-puckering taste
- The substances that give onions their characteristic smell, and eye-watering properties.

Some of them act as antioxidants, others have healthy hormone-like properties or have beneficial effects on our blood lipid (fat) levels.

Examples of phytochemicals

Allicin: An antioxidant from onions and garlic that helps protect the body's cells against harmful molecules called free radicals, thereby supporting the immune system and reducing the risk of chronic diseases such as clogged arteries, heart disease and cancer.

Anthocyanins: Antioxidant pigments found in purple, blue and black fruit and vegetables, such as beetroot and blueberries.

Bioflavonoids: Help with absorbing and protecting vitamin C. Citrus fruits are particularly rich in bioflavonoids.

Carotenoids: (Including beta-carotene, the pigment that makes carrots orange) are powerful antioxidants. At least forty carotenoids have been found in foods, and the best way of maximising your intake is to eat plenty of fruits and vegetables – especially the red, orange, yellow and green ones.

Flavonoids: Powerful antioxidants. They include the flavones (found in apple skins, onions, broccoli, grapes and olives) and flavanones (found in citrus fruits).

Isothiocyanates: Sulphur compounds found in vegetables such as Brussels sprouts and broccoli that help reduce the risk of cancer.

Lutein: A carotenoid worth special mention because of its importance for eye health. It's found in green leafy vegetables, and orange or yellow fruits and vegetables.

Lycopene: An even more potent antioxidant than beta-carotene. It's also linked with a reduction in prostate cancer risk. The best source of lycopene is tomatoes, but it's also found in pink grapefruits and apricots.

Phyto-oestrogens: These plant oestrogens were given their name because of their similarity to human oestrogens (female hormones). Scientific studies suggest that phyto-oestrogens could help prevent heart disease, as well as relieve menopausal symptoms. The main sources are soya products, but they are also found in flax seeds, sunflower seeds, pumpkin seeds, sesame seeds, lentils and chickpeas.

Phytosterols: These include stanols, which can help to reduce cholesterol levels.

4 Antioxidants

Antioxidants have become a nutrition buzzword, but why do we need them, and what are these 'oxidants' that they're 'anti'?

Oxidation is a process by which harmful molecules called free radicals damage our bodies' cells. Antioxidants protect us by reacting with the free radicals and mopping them up before they can cause this oxidative damage.

We can't avoid free radicals – they're produced naturally simply by living and breathing, and though factors such as cigarette smoke, pollution, burnt or charred food and excessive sun exposure add to our free radical burden. Free radical damage is implicated in a whole host of health problems, such as atherosclerosis (clogged arteries), heart disease, stroke, cancer and Alzheimer's disease. It even underlies the ageing process.

Many of the immune-boosting nutrients, such as vitamins A, C and E, also work as antioxidants, as do many phytochemicals.

These are some of the best antioxidant foods:

Fruit:
- Prunes
- Blueberries
- Blackberries
- Strawberries
- Raspberries
- Raisins
- Oranges
- Red grapes.

Vegetables:
- Kale
- Spinach
- Brussels sprouts
- Red peppers
- Onions.

Chocolate for health

Dark chocolate (with a high cocoa solids content) is often touted as a 'health food', thanks to its antioxidant content. Cocoa is rich in flavanols, and several studies have suggested that dark chocolate can decrease blood pressure and reduce the risk of clogged arteries, making it good for the heart. However, the devil is in the detail, and chocolate (even dark chocolate) is a high-sugar, high-fat food, so it's likely that the effects of these substances on your heart risk could more than outweigh the health-promoting effects of the flavanols. There are plenty of other, healthier foods that are rich in flavanols and other heart-healthy antioxidants, such as tea, fruit and vegetables. Also, many chocolate manufacturers use processes that destroy the flavanols, so you lose the antioxidant benefit. The bottom line is, keep an eye on any new research, but for now it would be unwise to think of chocolate as anything other than a treat that's may be slightly better for you than other sugary snacks.

Nutrients for colds

Sad to say, vitamin C can't prevent colds, but it could reduce their severity and duration. Drink orange juice, neat or diluted with hot water – it's appealing even when your taste buds are dulled by mucus. A mug of hot water with lemon juice and honey has a double action – the honey coats and soothes your throat, while the sharpness of the lemon stimulates saliva flow, adding its own soothing effect.

Zinc lozenges have an anti-viral action and can help to treat sore throats, but be careful not to take too much as this will actually suppress your immunity. When manufactured food is processed, its zinc content is drastically reduced – yet another reason to prepare more of your meals yourself.

Food, not supplements

Get your antioxidants from food, rather than pills. Population studies have revealed links between diets rich in antioxidants and better health, but most studies where people were given antioxidant tablets failed to produce the hoped-for benefits, and some even showed an increased risk of disease.

It seems that antioxidants work together in complex ways that scientists still don't fully understand, and antioxidant-rich foods harness these nutritious interactions in a way that cannot be bottled.

Body defence nutrients

Nutrient	Source
Vitamin A	Eggs; dairy products; oily fish; meat (especially liver)
Vitamin C	Citrus fruits; kiwi fruit; blackcurrants; strawberries; green vegetables (raw or lightly cooked)
Vitamin E	Nuts (especially almonds); seeds, and seed oils such as safflower and sunflower oil; avocados
Carotenoids	Carrots; red, orange and yellow peppers; sweet potatoes; dark green vegetables
Anthocyanins	Berries (especially blueberries); cherries; red grapes; red wine
Catechins	Green and black tea; dark chocolate (in moderation!)
Polyphenols	Dark chocolate; red wine – both in moderation!
Selenium	Brazil nuts; fish (especially shellfish); lamb; kidney and liver; egg yolks
Zinc	Lean meat (the richest source); seafood; dairy products. Vegan sources include chickpeas; pumpkin seeds and sunflower seeds; cashew and pecan nuts

5 Food and stress

Stress is an unavoidable part of modern life. A challenge can bring out the best in us, but that's not what we mean when we talk about 'stress'. It's the constant, chronic kind of stress that wears us down and threatens our health.

In an emergency, the body's stress response pumps out hormones that speed up our reactions, sharpen our senses and boost our endurance, hopefully getting us out of a tight situation. This is all well and good, but very often, modern stresses such as traffic jams, call-centre queues and money worries don't require us to spring into 'emergency mode', yet still the stress hormones are produced. Because the body believes this *could* be a matter of life or death, the stress reaction takes precedence over normal body processes like digestion and repair.

Stress can lead to:
- Headaches and migraines
- Anxiety/depression
- Insomnia
- Digestive problems such as stomach upsets
- Skin problems
- Suppression of the immune system
- Increased susceptibility to minor illnesses such as colds
- Increased risk of chronic diseases such as heart disease and cancer
- Raised blood pressure
- Increased pain from pre-existing conditions such as arthritis
- Missed periods (for women)
- Increased risk of chronic disease.

When we're stressed, and maintaining the body on a constant state of alert, we use up more nutrients than when we're coasting through life. And as our nutrient levels are depleted, our bodies find it harder and harder to cope with stress, leading to a downward spiral with symptoms such as tiredness, headaches and poor resistance to minor illnesses.

Stress also affects our digestion, and this makes us more prone to symptoms such as diarrhoea, constipation and irritable bowel syndrome before an important event or when we're under chronic stress. Also, stress can mean that we don't get the full benefit of the food we do eat – we need to digest our food properly in order to absorb the maximum nutrients from it.

Eating for stressful times
- Low-fat protein (concentrate on quality) from healthy sources such as fish, poultry, nuts and seeds, beans and lentils
- Complex starchy carbohydrates – stress increases your energy requirements, but you should get your calories from healthy sources. Fill up with wholemeal bread, brown pasta and noodles, brown rice, and other wholegrains such as oats, bulgur, buckwheat and millet
- Vitamin C – we use vitamin C more quickly when we're stressed, and it also helps support our immune systems. Vitamin C can't be stored in the body, so keep your levels topped up with citrus fruits, kiwi fruits, strawberries, blackberries, peppers and lightly cooked vegetables
- B vitamins – they're involved in releasing energy from our food, so help us to keep going when under pressure. You'll find them in wholegrains, meat, poultry, nuts and bananas.

> Some people turn to heavy drinking or smoking as a 'prop' when they're stressed. But as well as harming the body directly, these unhealthy habits also deplete nutrient levels even further.

Good nutrition is particularly important when we're under stress, but feeling under pressure can send our healthy eating intentions out of the window. Some people overeat (especially junk food). Others go off their food, and both of these reactions to stress mean our bodies don't get the

Stress-beating tips

■ Stress depletes your nutrient levels, so try not to let them get run down in the first place
■ Top up your 'stress nutrients' (see above)
■ Eat regularly and don't skip meals. This will help keep your blood sugar levels stable, and help you to resist unhealthy 'foody props' such as chocolate or crisps
■ Concentrate on low GI, 'slow fuel' food – once again, this will help keep your blood sugar levels, and your mood, on an even keel
■ Deal with any situations within your control, and for those you can't change, try relaxation techniques such as meditation or yoga.

nutrients they need, just when our nutritional needs are increased because of the additional demands stress places on our bodies.

When you are under stress (or short of time), concentrate on preparing simple, quick and nutritious meals rather than buying ready-meals, which are often high in fat and salt. Now is the time to take short cuts, fall back on your freezer and make use of a well-stocked store cupboard.

■ Buy ready prepared salad vegetables and vegetables that are washed, prepared and ready to be microwaved, steamed or baked
■ Buy meat and poultry that has been sliced into strips to make speedy stir-fries
■ Buy fresh soups (check the label for the salt content) to serve with crusty wholemeal rolls or bread
■ Keep your fruit bowl well stocked so you're not tempted to reach for a chocolate bar.

Keep your freezer stocked with:
■ A couple of kinds of vegetables – peas, sweetcorn and mixed vegetables freeze well
■ Some chicken breast fillets
■ Sustainably caught white fish and prawns
■ Fresh wholemeal breadcrumbs – for quick toppings to pasta and vegetables bakes, and fish
■ Lean minced meat or poultry – to make homemade burgers, meatballs and mince dishes
■ Individual portions of ready-to-heat rice to make risotto, kedgeree, rice salads or as an accompaniment to chilli con carne or curries. (Or buy 'express' rice in pouches to cook in the microwave.)
■ Healthy homemade pasta dishes such as lasagne, and pasta sauces.

6 Keeping your gut happy

Your gut is your body's food processor. You take in food, which is chopped up in the mouth, and in the stomach and intestine food is digested into simple molecules that the body can absorb and use. Then your gut gets rid of the waste material.

People often say 'you are what you eat'. It's a good analogy, but it's not the whole story. Actually, we are what we **digest and absorb**. Only food that's properly digested can be absorbed and used – otherwise it passes straight through our digestive system and we don't gain the benefit of its nutrients. So you can see why you need to be good to your gut.

Probably every one of us has been affected by digestive problems at some time, and more than one in three of us regularly suffer from digestive illnesses such as constipation, diarrhoea, irritable bowel syndrome (IBS), stomach-aches, nausea and sickness.

Fortunately, many of these illnesses can be prevented or relieved by controlling what we eat and when we eat it. Our lifestyle plays a part, too.

A healthy gut needs:
- Nutritious food
- Well-chewed food
- Plenty of fibre – something to 'work on'
- Plenty of water
- A good balance of 'friendly bacteria' in the gut
- Plenty of exercise to help keep the gut moving.

Your digestive system doesn't need:
- Stress
- Fatty foods
- Too much alcohol
- 'Trigger foods' – these vary between people, but include coffee, spicy foods and acidic foods
- A lazy lifestyle
- For you to smoke
- Late suppers.

Know your trigger foods

Most of us have at least one food that 'disagrees' with us, causing symptoms from embarrassing gurgling or wind, to diarrhoea or bloating. Trigger foods can also contribute to IBS. Fatty foods are a problem for many of us. Other common trigger foods include spicy foods (such as curries), onions and garlic, alcohol or coffee. The best solution is to learn what your 'triggers' are, and then avoid them.

Friendly bacteria

Our intestines are inhabited by millions of bacteria. There are hundreds of species living inside us, and fortunately most are protective – our so-called 'friendly bacteria'. It's a competitive world in the gut, with a constant battle between the beneficial bacteria and less friendly bugs that could make you ill. What you want to achieve is a flourishing population of 'good' bacteria, which can crowd the harmful germs out.

Ideally, you'll have a good population of beneficial bacteria, keeping the bad bugs' population down. But a poor diet, stress, illnesses such as diarrhoea, and especially taking antibiotic medication (which kills bacteria indiscriminately) can upset the balance. If the harmful bacteria multiply enough to get the upper hand, they crowd out the beneficial bacteria we need in order to feel at our best.

There are two ways of tipping the balance in favour of the friendly bacteria. Probiotics and prebiotics both aim to help the friendly bacteria, but in different ways.

Probiotics

Probiotics are actual bacteria, the beneficial ones. You can get these in supplement form (capsules or powder) or in little pots of probiotic drinks and yogurts. When buying a supplement, look for one with the maximum number of 'viable organisms' – that's the living bugs.

Probiotic supplements and foods attempt to tip the balance in your gut in favour of the beneficial bugs by boosting their numbers. The problem with this is the difficult journey the bacteria face in order to reach their final home in your intestines. On the way, they have to pass through the highly acidic conditions of the stomach, and some studies suggest that many of the bacteria are killed before reaching and colonising the bowel, their intended destination.

If your gut is healthy, with a good population of probiotics already living there, taking supplementary bugs is unlikely to make you feel any better. But if you suffer from a disorder

such as IBS, or are taking antibiotics, probiotics are definitely worth a try. (Leave at least two hours between the antibiotics and the probiotics, and take them with food.)

As well as keeping the harmful bugs down, probiotic bacteria also manufacture small but useful amounts of vitamin K and vitamin B_{12}, supplementing what you get from your diet. Friendly bacteria also ferment soluble fibre from your diet to produce so-called short-chain fatty acids, which nourish the cells of the large intestine and aid healing of the gut, as well as reducing the risk of bowel cancer.

As well as probiotics, there's another kind of 'bacteria booster' for your intestines that probably has more potential for keeping your friendly bacteria flourishing.

Prebiotics

You can buy several kinds of prebiotic supplements, as well as products containing prebiotics, including yogurt drinks, bread and breakfast cereals.

Prebiotics aren't bacteria, they're 'bacteria food' that helps the friendly (probiotic) bacteria inside you to flourish. Prebiotics are useless to the harmful germs in your gut, and we can't digest them either – only the beneficial bacteria can use them, and this exclusive food supply gives them a big advantage.

Another factor in favour of prebiotics is the fact that because they're not 'alive', they can't be killed by the acidic conditions in the stomach or the powerful digestive enzymes throughout the digestive system. Prebiotics pass through the gut and reach the friendly bacteria unharmed.

Know your prebiotics

Some foods have a prebiotic effect – bananas, artichokes, onions and leeks are particularly useful sources. Other kinds of prebiotic you may have seen in supplement form and on ingredients lists are inulin and fructo-oligo-saccharides (FOS).

What can go wrong with the gut
Diarrhoea
Diarrhoea occurs when the body doesn't absorb enough water from the waste products in the digestive system, so the 'end product' is runny and watery. It can be caused by infections ('tummy bugs'), by irritation of the gut (for example by 'trigger foods' that disagree with you), and also by stress and anxiety.

If you're down with diarrhoea, don't worry if you don't feel like eating – it's much more important to keep hydrated with plenty of water to replace the fluids you're losing.

Once you can face food again, try bland starchy carbohydrates, such as a dry cream cracker, a rice cake, a piece of dry toast or some plain boiled rice, while your digestive system recovers. Avoid fatty or dairy foods, alcohol, coffee and caffeinated soft drinks until your digestion is completely back to normal. It's also a good idea not to eat too much high-fibre food (such as fruit and vegetables) for a while.

Once you're feeling better, you could consider bio-yogurt, or a probiotic supplement, to help replenish your beneficial gut bacteria.

Constipation
The main causes of constipation are:
- Not enough fluids
- Not enough fibre.

Fluids and fibre provide 'bulk' for the gut to work on. Food moves along the digestive system by means of muscular contractions, rather like squeezing toothpaste along a flexible rubber tube. It's easier to squeeze along if there's plenty of substance to squeeze, and it's not too dry.

Exercise helps prevent constipation, too, by stimulating the gut to keep moving.

> Don't be tempted to suddenly increase the fibre in your diet – this can actually cause diarrhoea *or* constipation, as it can irritate the gut. Instead, gradually increase your fibre intake, to allow the digestive system to adapt and get used to the change.

Indigestion
Indigestion occurs when the stomach's acidic contents escape and rise up into the oesophagus, and sometimes as far as the throat or mouth, causing a burning sensation or an acidic taste. A burning feeling behind the breastbone is referred to as heartburn.

It's generally brought on by eating too much,

or rich food, or certain foods that irritate your stomach. Some medications cause indigestion as a side effect, and it can also be a symptom of a stomach ulcer.

Tips to relieve indigestion:
- Avoid large meals, or wolfing down your food. Chew your food thoroughly
- Avoid foods you know to be 'triggers' for you. The commonest culprits are fatty foods, spicy foods, caffeine, and acidic foods such as vinegar, strawberries or citrus fruit
- Eat small, regular meals that are not too fatty
- Don't eat late at night, and don't lie down or exercise straight after eating
- Try to reduce the stress in your life
- Avoid taking aspirin or ibuprofen (unless advised by your doctor) as these can irritate the stomach.

If indigestion persists for more than a couple of weeks, or if it worsens, you should see your GP.

Irritable bowel syndrome

In irritable bowel syndrome (IBS), the gut becomes hypersensitive. The normal movement of food through the digestive system is disrupted, causing the gut to go into spasms. The digestive system is then unable to digest or absorb food properly.

Symptoms include pain in the abdomen, nausea, bloating, wind, constipation, diarrhoea (or alternation between the two), having to rush to the toilet, lethargy and headaches.

It can be a very distressing and painful condition. People's symptoms vary enormously, suggesting that the causes are likewise varied. Medication is available to help with the spasms. Your doctor will also be able to help you to identify the things which make your condition better or worse.

Once again, many people have 'trigger foods', such as onions, wheat products, citrus fruits or caffeine. Very high-fibre diets can also make IBS worse.

Twelve tips for a healthy digestive system

1. Eat plenty of fibre, both soluble and insoluble kinds, and aim to have some high-fibre food with every meal. That means plenty of wholegrains, pulses (beans and lentils), fruit and vegetables.

2. Cut out your trigger foods – avoid spicy foods, coffee and fizzy drinks if they're a problem for you.

3. Cut down on fatty foods, especially fast food. Too much fat isn't good for you anyway, and it's hard for your digestive system to handle.

4. Make sure that you get enough fluids, and preferably pure water. Fizzy drinks are a bad idea!

5. Consider prebiotics, and possibly probiotics, if you are taking antibiotics or your digestive system is under stress.

6. Don't drink too much alcohol. That's no more than 2–3 units of alcohol a day for women, and 3–4 units for men, with some alcohol-free days each week. Drinking more than this can irritate the gut and inhibit nutrient absorption and use.

7. Chew your food well – good digestion begins in the mouth.

8. Eat sitting at the table, rather than standing up in the kitchen, on a tray on your lap, or lying on the floor. Concentrate on your food, rather than reading or watching television.

9. Make time for proper mealtimes and don't bolt your food – take time to relax and chew properly.

10. Don't lie down for half an hour after eating.

11. Don't exercise for at least an hour after eating.

12. Stress contributes to many digestive problems, so try to learn how to manage it.

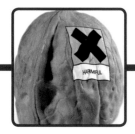

7 Allergies and intolerances

As many as one in five people believe that they are intolerant or allergic to a food, but in fact, less than one per cent of the UK's adult population have a true food allergy. The figure is higher for children (up to five per cent), but many of these grow out of the condition.

True allergies are serious, and can even be life-threatening, while severe intolerances can cause intense and uncomfortable symptoms. However, self-diagnosing and removing foods or food groups from your diet can leave your diet seriously lacking in vital nutrients.

Allergies

Allergies occur when your body's immune system is confused into launching an exaggerated immune response to a harmless food, as if it was a dangerous substance or germ.

Symptoms include rashes, swelling, itchy skin, diarrhoea and other digestive upsets.

Anaphylaxis (or anaphylactic shock) is a potentially life-threatening allergic reaction where the airways swell, restricting breathing. People who know that this serious reaction could happen to them must avoid the offending food(s). In case they accidentally eat something containing the food, their doctor will usually give them a special 'pen' to inject themselves with a drug to open up the airways as soon they notice the symptoms.

Nuts (especially peanuts) account for most severe cases of food allergy and anaphylaxis, but other common food allergens include cows' milk, eggs, soya products (including soya milk), fish and shellfish, fruit (especially bananas, apples, citrus fruit, peaches and plums), seeds, and herbs and spices.

The only reliable way to diagnose food allergies is an allergy test, which detects antibodies in the blood. This is available from your GP. If this is positive, you can be referred to a dietitian, or other registered nutrition professional, to help you to devise a diet that avoids the foods you are allergic to, but still provides all the nutrients you need.

Intolerances

Intolerances are similar to allergies, but there are several important differences:

- They are usually not dangerous
- They are caused by your body not producing enough of the particular enzymes or compounds needed to digest and absorb the food
- Symptoms are slower to appear
- Symptoms tend to be more 'vague', affecting more than one body system. They include headaches, bloating, lethargy, and aches and pains
- They are harder to diagnose than allergies.

Food intolerances are far more common than allergies – up to 20 per cent of us have problems of some kind with one or more foods.

Intolerances are difficult to diagnose, because their symptoms don't appear for several hours or even days. The symptoms are extremely variable, both in their nature and severity. For some people, intolerances can cause severe symptoms

that disrupt their lives, while for others the symptoms are hardly noticeable. The quantity of food that it takes to cause problems also varies – sometimes you can get away with eating just a little.

The foods most commonly causing intolerances are: cheese, yeast extract, red wine, chocolate, fruits, caffeine-containing foods, wheat and some food additives (such as sulphur dioxide and sulphites).

Previously, despite the presence of a huge variety of so-called food intolerance tests on the market, the only reliable way to diagnose intolerances was to keep a 'food diary' and remove the suspect food to see if symptoms reduced or disappeared over several weeks. More reliable blood tests are being developed, but there are still many suspect tests on the market, and you should ask a registered health professional for advice before parting with any

Coeliac disease

Coeliac disease is caused by a reaction to the protein gluten, which is found in wheat and also other grains such as barley, rye and oats. The protein reaction damages the lining of the small intestine, and this leads to nutrients not being properly absorbed, as well as symptoms such as pain and diarrhoea. Coeliac disease is diagnosed by a blood test, and if this is positive, sufferers will need to follow a gluten-free diet for life.

money or changing your diet. You should also be wary of jumping to conclusions or making assumptions that a particular food is behind your symptoms. If you plan to 'test-remove' any major food groups, such as dairy or wheat, you should ask your GP to refer you to a registered nutrition professional for advice.

8 Reducing your disease risk

A poor diet will age you before your time, hindering your immune system, and putting you more at risk of the diseases that could cut your life short. On the other hand, a healthy diet can reduce your risk, helping you to live longer and healthier.

Eating healthily can reduce your risk of:
- Obesity
- High blood pressure
- Clogged arteries (atherosclerosis)
- Heart disease
- Stroke
- Cancer
- Osteoporosis
- Type 2 diabetes
- Dental problems
- Osteoarthritis
- Depression.

Reduce your risk: heart disease

Heart disease usually goes hand in hand with high blood pressure and atherosclerosis (arteries clogged with cholesterol deposits). People with type 2 diabetes generally have raised blood pressure and cholesterol levels, so this condition also increases their heart risk.

High blood pressure puts a strain on the heart and damages blood vessels, while narrowed arteries make it harder for blood to reach every part of our bodies. Since it's blood that transports nutrients and oxygen to our cells, an interruption in blood supply can damage the cells, and even cause them to die.

An interruption to the heart's blood supply causes a heart attack. So you can see why it's important to keep your blood pressure down, and your blood vessels clear and smooth.

Watch your weight: Being overweight or obese increases your cardiovascular risk.

Eat fruit and vegetables: They're rich in antioxidants, which help reduce the risk of atherosclerosis.

Reduce salt: It can increase your blood pressure.

Eat beans and lentils: They're extremely low in saturated fat and high in soluble fibre, which 'mops up' harmful cholesterol.

Eat oily fish: It's rich in omega-3 essential fatty acids, which improve your cholesterol balance and reduce the risk of dangerous blood clots.

Replace saturated fats with healthier unsaturated fats (polyunsaturates and monounsaturates) to reduce your risk of atherosclerosis. Monounsaturates, such as olive oil, are particularly good at lowering 'bad' LDL-cholesterol levels.

Eat nuts: They contain monounsaturated fats (beneficial for cholesterol levels) and antioxidant vitamin E. Vitamin E-rich foods appear to be particularly effective against heart disease.

Moderate your fat intake: A diet high in fat (from any source, including the healthy ones) increases your risk of becoming overweight.

Eat wholegrains: Fibre-rich wholegrains help weight control by filling you up and balancing your blood sugar levels.

Eat oats: They're especially good for your heart, thanks to the soluble fibre that mops up excess dietary cholesterol.

Drink wine (in moderation) and tea: The polyphenols they contain lower your LDL-cholesterol level, reduce your risk of dangerous blood clots and act as antioxidants, protecting your blood vessels.

Soya protein: Research suggests that replacing animal protein with 50 grams of soya protein a day can reduce your 'bad' LDL-cholesterol and increase 'good' HDL-cholesterol.

Tips for getting soya into your diet:

- Use soya mince to make Bolognese sauces, chilli 'non' carne and cottage pies
- Marinate tofu and use in stir-fries
- Used tinned or frozen soya beans in stews and casseroles
- Serve soya ice cream or yogurt with fresh fruit for dessert
- Whizz up a banana and berries with soya milk to make a nutritious smoothie
- Use soya milk on your breakfast cereal
- Ask for your latte or cappuccino to be made with soya milk.

Reduce your risk: strokes

In terms of diet and lifestyle, it's safe to say that what's good for your heart is good for your brain as well. The brain depends on a healthy blood supply to provide it with oxygen and nutrients. In effect, a stroke is a 'brain attack'. An interruption in the blood supply to the brain (caused by a blood clot or a burst blood vessel) leads to damage and the death of brain cells.

Most of the lifestyle factors that harm our brains do so through their effect on our arteries. Probably the best thing you can do for your brain is keep these blood vessels in good condition. This means that all the advice on a heart-healthy diet (above) will lower your stroke risk as well. Foods high in saturated fat raise your levels of LDL-cholesterol, lower your HDL-cholesterol, and lead to clogged and damaged arteries – in the brain as well as the rest of the body. Keeping your blood pressure down will also lower your stroke risk.

Reduce your risk: cancer

It's estimated that up to a third of cancer cases (especially breast, bowel, stomach and oesophageal cancer) could be prevented by healthy diets.

Stay a healthy weight: Being overweight can increase your risk of breast and endometrial cancer, among others.

Eat plenty of fruit and vegetables: They can reduce your risk of many cancers, especially those affecting the digestive system (for example, oesophageal, stomach and bowel cancers).

Eat high-fibre foods: A high-fibre diet can reduce your bowel cancer risk, as well as helping you to maintain a healthy weight. It seems that insoluble fibre (from wholegrains, fruit and vegetables) bulks up the contents of your digestive system and smoothes it through your bowels, reducing the amount of time that potential carcinogens (cancer-causing chemicals) spend in contact with your bowel walls. Soluble fibre (from oats, pulses, fruit and vegetables) help to feed 'friendly bacteria' in the bowel that produce chemicals that help prevent tumours from developing. Fruit and vegetables are high in fibre. Pulses and wholegrains are also good sources.

Reduce processed and red meat, and charred foods: Reduce your intake of red meats such as beef, lamb and pork, and especially of processed meat products such as sausages, salami, ham and bacon, as these can increase your risk of bowel and possibly stomach cancer. Replace them with other protein sources such as poultry, fish, eggs and pulses. Reducing your red and processed meat intake will also mean you eat less fat. Cooking food until it chars (as in barbecuing) can produce cancer-causing chemicals – moist cooking methods such as steaming, braising and casseroling are healthier.

Reduce fatty foods: A high-fat diet (especially saturated fat and hydrogenated fats) is associated with a greater risk of cancers, including breast cancer.

Cut down on salty foods: They can increase your risk of stomach cancer.

Drink only moderately: Too much alcohol has been linked with an increased risk of mouth, liver, throat and breast cancer.

Cancer-fighting foods

Foods such as fruit, vegetables, nuts and seeds are linked with a lower risk of cancer. This is probably due to the phytochemicals and antioxidants they contain, as well as their fibre content.

Cruciferous vegetables (such as Brussels sprouts, broccoli, cabbage and cauliflower) contain cancer-fighting phytochemicals called glucosinolates.

Orange and yellow fruit and vegetables are rich in antioxidant carotenoids such as beta-carotene, which appear to reduce the risk of damage to DNA that can trigger cancer.

Dark coloured fruits, especially berries, contain antioxidant pigments called anthocyanins.

Tomatoes contain lycopene, which is an antioxidant. Some research suggests that it is particularly effective against prostate cancer.

Nuts and seeds are high in antioxidant vitamin E, which can help prevent the damage to cells that triggers cancer. Flaxseeds contain phytochemicals called lignins, which could reduce your risk of breast, prostate and bowel cancer. Brazil nuts are rich in selenium, which acts as an antioxidant.

Tea contains phytochemicals including polyphenols, which could reduce the risk of cancers, including stomach cancer.

However, you should get your cancer-fighters from food, not pills, as studies show that supplements of individual antioxidant nutrients are not effective and can actually increase cancer risk.

Reduce your risk: type 2 diabetes

Much of the alarming increase in type 2 diabetes can be blamed on unhealthy diets.

If you want to reduce your risk, the best thing you can do get down to a healthy weight if you're overweight.

- Concentrate on low glycaemic index (GI) foods, to sustain you and balance your blood sugar levels.
- Make sure your diet isn't too high in fat, as fat is the most calorific nutrient. Try to ensure that most of the fat you do eat is the healthy unsaturated kind, rather than saturated or hydrogenated fat.
- Eat plenty of fibre-rich foods.
- Replace red meat with poultry, fish, beans and lentils – this will reduce the fat you eat and increase your fibre intake.
- Snack on a variety of fruit and vegetables.

As well as helping you to lose weight, increasing your exercise reduces your type 2 diabetes risk through its effect on blood sugar control.

Reduce your risk: osteoporosis

Although the key period for building up your maximum bone density (therefore reducing your osteoporosis risk later in life) is the years up to the early thirties, you shouldn't neglect your bone-building and bone-maintaining nutrients after this stage.

Eat plenty of calcium-rich foods, such as low-fat dairy products, tofu, fish where the soft bones are eaten, broccoli, and sesame seeds.

Get adequate vitamin D from exposure to sunshine and enriched low-fat spreads.

Reduce your salt intake. Salt appears to increase calcium excretion from the body.

Avoid heavy drinking. Too much alcohol has a negative effect on bone-building hormones and cells.

Avoid being underweight. Being underweight significantly increases your osteoporosis risk.

Plenty of weight-bearing exercise (such as walking, jogging and weight-training), and not smoking, will also lower your osteoporosis risk.

Reduce your risk: brain ageing and Alzheimer's disease

Much of the way your brain ages is down to genetics. But a healthy diet, rich in 'brain-friendly' food (in other words, foods that help keep our blood vessels healthy, see Reduce your risk: heart disease), could go a long way towards holding back the 'mental slow-down' we associate with old age.

Although the evidence is less clear-cut than that for diet reducing stroke risk, it appears that a brain-friendly diet could even reduce the risk of dementias, such as Alzheimer's disease. Doctors are finding that many people diagnosed with Alzheimer's also have brain changes related to blood vessel problems. Studies also suggest that high cholesterol increases your risk of developing Alzheimer's, and even that cholesterol could have a direct effect on the brain.

It is also thought that some foods may have a protective effect against Alzheimer's, as well as age-related 'mental slow-down'.

■ **Omega-3s**: These essential fatty acids (EFAs), found in oily fish, and some nuts and seeds, appear to reduce your risk. Omega-6 EFAs don't have the same effect.
■ **Vegetables**: Packed with antioxidants and folic acid, which help protect the blood vessels. Green leafy vegetables appear to have the strongest effect.
■ **Fruit**: Another great antioxidant source, though the research supporting their effect versus brain-ageing and Alzheimer's is less convincing than for vegetables.
■ **Green and white tea**: Research found that Japanese people drinking more than two cups of green tea a day had a 50 per cent

lower chance of mental decline than those who drunk less green tea. It appears to be the catechins in the tea that provide the benefit.
■ **Concord grape juice**: This contains similar polyphenols to those in tea, and could also help slow brain-ageing. New research suggests that apple juice (and apples) could have a similar effect.

Coffee for your brain

A study in elderly men found that drinking three cups of coffee a day reduced their risk of developing Alzheimer's disease. While more research needs to be done before coffee could be recommended for this, it adds weight to the argument that coffee is not a 'toxin' and could actually be good for us in moderation.

Maintain a healthy weight

Maintaining a healthy weight appears to lower your risk of brain problems later in life. Being obese, and particularly having a large waist measurement, is associated with an increased risk of Alzheimer's disease.

Chapter 6

Food and mood

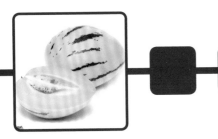

It's impossible to untangle food and mood.

The way we feel affects what we eat:
- We 'comfort eat' when we feel miserable
- We lose our appetite when under stress
- We find it harder to resist temptation when we're feeling down
- We may feel eating healthier is easier when we're feeling positive.

What we eat affects the way we feel:
- Stimulant foods (such as coffee) make us feel alert, and possibly anxious
- Sugary, high glycaemic index (GI) foods give us a brief burst of energy
- Heavy meals can make us feel sluggish
- The lack of certain nutrients can make us feel below par and can lead to deficiencies, which can affect our emotions.

Even marginal nutrient deficiencies can have psychological effects, generally making us feel low or depressed.

These are the nutrients most commonly linked with mood, so pay particular attention to your intake of foods rich in:

- Selenium
- Iron
- Vitamin C
- Thiamin (vitamin B1)
- Riboflavin (vitamin B2)
- Folic acid
- Omega-3 essential fatty acids.

(For good sources of these nutrients, see Chapter 2.)

Feel good with fish

Population studies have found that countries where people eat a lot of oily fish (the best source of omega-3 essential fatty acids) have particularly low rates of depression. And medical trials of high-dose omega-3s have shown encouraging results in improving symptoms of depression.

It certainly looks as though omega-3s are involved in good moods, so it makes sense to boost your intake of these beneficial fats, found mainly in oily fish, but also in flax seeds and flax seed oil.

1 Blood sugar and mood

Our blood sugar can affect our mood. Unless we suffer from diabetes, our sugar regulation system works like a thermostat, keeping our blood glucose levels within safe levels. Although our blood sugar will rise and fall at a rate determined by what we eat (the amount and its glycaemic index), it cannot rise too high or fall too low to harm us.

However, many people can 'feel' when their blood sugar levels rise and fall, even within these set limits. When they eat something sugary they get a buzz, as their blood sugar level rises. But soon the glucose is used up or squirreled away in their body's cells, their blood glucose levels fall, and they feel their energy levels plummeting. And all too often, this is accompanied by mood swings. If this is you, it's especially important for you to maintain steady blood sugar levels by eating low glycaemic index (GI) foods (see Chapter 7).

2 Stimulant foods

Constituents of some foods and drinks, such as the caffeine in coffee, cola and chocolate, have a stimulant effect. As well as acting directly on our brains, they also cause a quick spike in our blood glucose levels.

This means that they make you feel more alert in the short term, and so may be useful before an exam or job interview, and can relieve tiredness temporarily. But in effect it's 'false energy', and they don't provide the kind of steady blood sugar levels associated with sustained energy and stable moods.

The chocolate effect

Chocolate has been touted as having 'drug-like' effects on the brain, and the phrase 'chocoholic' is often quoted. Chocolate does contain chemicals called anadamides, which act on the same area of the brain as drugs such as cannabis, but it appears that you'd have to eat enormous amounts of chocolate in order to achieve a drug-like effect.

So why does chocolate feel so 'addictive'? It's probably because eating any food that we find so desirable and enjoyable to eat lights up the same 'pleasure centres' in the brain as drugs, stimulating the release of the 'happy chemicals' known as endorphins.

Other enemies of calm moods and stable blood sugar levels

- Skipping meals
- Alcohol
- Caffeine
- Stress
- Cigarettes.

3 Food and psychology

Food is an intensely psychological topic. We form extremely strong emotional associations with foods. The way foods make us feel also affects our liking for them.

Comfort foods

Our minds link ice cream and sweets with happy childhood memories, associate caramel lattes and muffins with relaxing during a shopping trip, and connect cakes with celebrations. Because of this, our brains file these foods away as 'feel-good foods'. Whenever we eat them, we expect to feel better, and so we do. And each time this happens, the link is reinforced.

Stimulant foods and 'sick-making' foods

Research has shown that pairing caffeine (which makes people feel alert) with a fruity drink increases their liking for that drink, because they associate it with feeling alert and 'good'. And after a bad experience with a food, like some seafood that leads to a tummy upset, that food may always turn your stomach. (However, this doesn't always hold true – someone may suffer a bad reaction to strawberries or oranges for example, but still enjoy eating them all the same.)

Avoiding food that could potentially make us ill is all very well. And it would be fine if our feel-good foods were apples and broccoli. But unfortunately when we turn to food for comfort, it's more likely to be high in fat and sugar, and low in nutrients.

4 Snacking

Snacks receive a lot of bad press, but it's not snacking that's bad for you, it's what you snack on!

Chosen wisely, snacks can help to sustain you between meals without succumbing to the temptation of unhealthier pit-stops, as well as helping you to reach your nutrient targets for the day.

What makes a good snack?
- It should be sustaining enough to keep you going until the next meal (protein–carbohydrate combinations are particularly good)
- It should be 'nutrient dense' – the maximum nutrition in a small package
- It should be low in fat, salt and sugar
- It should be easy-to-eat, preferably with your fingers
- It should be portable, if you need to take it out, or pack it in a lunch box
- It should ideally contain two out of the following three:
  - Fruit/vegetables
  - Protein: nuts, cheese, milk, yoghurt, or meat
  - Starchy carbohydrate.

Choose snacks that hit the spot

Some people are sweet snackers, some prefer savoury, but most of us are a combination – and we prefer different snacks at different times.

When you're trying to swap a healthy snack for a less healthy one, try to substitute like for like. If you try to swap some celery sticks (savoury and crunchy) for an ice cream (sweet and creamy) you'll feel cheated, and will probably end up eating the unhealthy snack as well!

Good snack swaps:
Instead of these sweet snacks:
- Cakes
- Sweet biscuits
- Danish pastries
- Ice cream.

Have these healthier substitutes:
- Scones (preferably wholemeal)
- Homemade cakes and bakes, low in fat and sugar
- Currant buns
- Malt loaf
- Healthier biscuits (see box)
- Small bowl of wholegrain cereal with semi-skimmed milk
- A slice of wholemeal bread made into a sandwich with low-fat cream cheese and a tiny bit of honey
- A toasted wholemeal English muffin with honey or pure fruit spread.

Instead of these confectionary snacks:
- Chocolate
- Sweets.

Have these healthier alternatives:
- Dried fruit and unsalted nuts
- Fresh fruit.

Instead of these creamy snacks:
- Ice cream
- Trifles
- Creamy desserts.

Have these healthier alternatives:
- Low-fat yogurt or fromage frais (preferably natural yogurt with fruit swirled in)
- Frozen yogurt
- Low-fat rice pudding
- Fruit smoothies made from frozen berries and low-fat natural yogurt.

Instead of these savoury snacks:
- Crisps, tortilla chips
- Peanuts, salted nuts.

Have these healthier alternatives:
- Veggie sticks and a dip (cottage cheese, salsa, or a low-fat cream cheese dip)
- Oatcakes (with cottage cheese if you like)
- Breadsticks (with a healthy dip if you like)
- Rice cakes (with a healthy topping if you like)
- Plain popcorn (try adding some paprika or black pepper)
- Wholemeal toast with a thin spread of peanut butter
- Wholewheat crackers with a healthy topping
- Pretzels or baked (not fried) crisps (occasionally, as they are generally high in salt).

Of course, there's no need to ban the less healthy snacks totally. Just make sure that foods such as chocolate bars, crisps and cakes are occasional treats, not part of your everyday diet.

'Healthier biscuits'

Is there such a thing as a healthy biscuit? Well, oatcakes certainly come close (high in fibre and low in fat and sugar), but they're not the kind of thing you'd want to dunk in your tea!

If you *must* have a biscuit, these are the 'least bad' options – the ones that are lowest in calories, fat and sugar.
- Fig rolls
- Digestive biscuits
- Garibaldi biscuits
- Plain biscuits (eg Marie, Rich Tea and Arrowroot)
- Jaffa cakes or gingersnaps (low in calories and fat, but high in sugar).

Vary your snacks – have a mixture of fruit, nuts, carbohydrates, dairy, etc. That way you'll increase the variety of nutrients you're incorporating in your diet, helping you to hit your nutrient targets.

Super-snacks: the protein–carbohydrate combo

Combining protein with a carbohydrate snack lowers the snack's glycaemic index (GI), making it extra-sustaining and even more effective at helping you to keep going until the next meal.

Examples include:
- Dried fruit + unsalted nuts or a small piece of cheese
- Fresh fruit salad + a sprinkling of seeds
- Half a multigrain bagel + low-fat cream cheese
- Smoothie made from fruit + low-fat natural yogurt
- A scone or currant bun + a glass of semi-skimmed milk
- A slice of bread with a scrape of olive-oil spread + a hard-boiled egg.

5 Cravings

All humans, at least when they're born, are 'hard-wired' with the same biological food cravings. We evolved to seek out these foods, because they contain nutrients our bodies need:

Salt: Needed to maintain our body's fluid balance, and for the transmission of impulses along nerves.

Fat: The most concentrated source of energy (calories).

Sugar: Another source of energy in an extremely 'quick-release' form.

In the kind of small doses our ancestors would have eaten, these kinds of foods are essential. But nowadays, with foods packed with fat, sugar and salt so cheap and available, it's all too easy to 'overdose' on them, leading to us piling on the pounds and increasing our risk of chronic health problems.

What do we crave?

The foods we crave tend to be high in carbohydrates (especially refined carbohydrates and sugar), and to a lesser extent, fat and salt. Interestingly, men are more likely to crave fatty, salty foods (such as chips and crisps), while woman yearn more for sweet foods such as chocolate (the number one food craving).

A craving for sugar could be down to the body's need for quickly available sugar, though because we can make our own sugar by breaking down more complex carbohydrates or releasing it from body stores, obviously this isn't the whole story. Once again it appears that psychology plays a role. Sugary foods are so enjoyable, they cause the pleasure centres in the brain to light up and endorphins ('happy chemicals') to be released. It's not so much the food itself we crave, but its effect on our brains. And every time we get that happy feeling after eating ice cream, the craving is reinforced.

We also tend to experience stronger cravings, which are harder to resist, when we're under stress. This ties in with a need for instant energy, combined with a feeling that we need our 'reward foods', and that drug-like effect created by endorphins in the brain that makes us feel better, albeit temporarily.

Dieting also strengthens cravings. We're hungry, our energy levels are likely to be low, and we'll probably be missing our favourite foods. Studies have shown that being deprived of a food only intensifies our desire for it.

Following a very low-calorie or 'fad' diet that leaves us deficient in essential nutrients will also affect our moods, making us more likely to succumb to unhealthy cravings. This in turn makes us feel guilty – it's not a healthy pattern to get in to.

Coping with cravings

Succumbing to the occasional chocolate biscuit or slice of cake isn't the end of the world. If the occasional cappuccino and a muffin is what it

takes to keep you on an even keel, then so be it. But constantly giving in to unhealthy cravings can seriously unbalance your diet – moderation is the key.

Try these tips to stay in control:
- Keep your blood sugar levels stable with low-GI foods, by eating low-GI meals based around low-fat protein, wholegrains and potatoes, and plenty of vegetables
- Keep up your energy levels with low-GI snacks such as fruit, veggie sticks, unsalted nuts and high-fibre carbohydrates, such as oatcakes
- Try to include protein with every meal – it will lower the glycaemic index of the meal and sustain you for longer
- Don't skip meals
- Don't go on fad diets

- Take some exercise. It'll take your mind off the craving, and also stimulate the release of endorphins
- Try to satisfy your craving with a healthier alternative (see Snacking, earlier in this chapter). If you need something sweet, try a piece of fruit or a small quantity of dried fruit
- Don't completely ban foods. If a food is totally off-limits and you give in to temptation, you're more likely to go overboard and gorge yourself on it
- Limit your portions. Rather than wolfing down an entire bar of chocolate, take out just a square or two, then wrap up the rest and put it out of sight
- If chocolate is your weakness, stick to good quality, high cocoa solids chocolate. You'll get an intense cocoa hit, with less sugar and fat, and fewer calories.